A Journey to Enlightenment – Kundalini Rising

By Maria Lobato

© Copyright 2023 - All rights reserved.

The content contained within this book may not be reproduced, duplicated, or transmitted without direct written permission from the author or the publisher.

Under no circumstances will any blame or legal responsibility be held against the publisher, or author, for any damages, reparation, or monetary loss due to the information contained within this book, either directly or indirectly.

Cover picture by Prakash Yalamarthi.

About the author

A Spiritual Medium since birth, a Life and Spiritual Coach, NLP Master Practitioner, Hypnotherapist and Healer, Maria focus her many talents helping people transform into their better versions and move forward in life with confidence and self-esteem. Maria is a guide and mentor taking people into deep journeys of self-development, spiritual awakenings and helping them navigate the dark night of the Soul.

Author of "A journey to self-love", "Illusion", "Awakening", "Revelations" Enlightenment", "All about Spirit Guides" and co-author of the Best Sellers "Everyday Women's Guide to Doing What You Love" and "Everyday Woman's Guide to Success in your Business", Maria keeps inspiring people in many ways.

"I am someone who has been in the nitty gritty of life, just like you."

To my guides and spiritual helpers,
For their unconditional love, support, and guidance.

Table of Contents

Introduction 1

In the beginning 3

The Goddess 8

The Ego's Death 14

The Awakening 17

Kundalini 21

Back into life 24

Attachments 27

The Heart 32

Facing the shadow 35

Contemplating 39

Perfection 41

Thoughts 43

Work 45

Suffering 49

Sexuality 51

The Crown 55

Trust Shakti. Shakti knows 59

Kali 62

Energy 67

Enlightenment 71

Self-Identification 74

Meaning 77

Devotion 80

The nervous system 83

The Higher Heart 85

This is just the beginning 90

Introduction

How did I get here?

Jobless, alone, soon to lose my house, broke, middle-aged woman.

I have nothing to show for, let my bank account serve as a witness, but still I have never felt happier.

I wake up every day with this sense of peace and well-being that I have never felt before.

- -

I wrote the above about 6 months ago, on the day I decided to start this book. Since then, many things changed in my life, but the biggest changes were felt in the core of my being.

This book is an account of my experience following a Kundalini activation. I documented every step of the process as I felt this was a journey I would one day like to share with others. Almost 3 years down the line, the desire to share became very strong and I embarked on the adventure of writing this book.

Although my awakening was fuelled by the Kundalini energy, the goddess Shakti herself, the steps I went through and describe in this book are common to most spiritual awakenings. The losses, the doubts, the realizations, and the liberation, they are all part of the self-realization path. With or without the Kundalini activation.

It is my intention that this book can bring you comfort, knowledge and guidance so that your spiritual awakening can be a little easier than mine was.

We are all in this together, my heart goes out to meet yours.

What if we rewind a bit and I tell you exactly how I got here?

In the beginning

The love was gone, and I could not remain in a failed marriage any more. It had been wrong from day one, but I decided to ignore my intuition and push through. For years, I ignored the loud screams of my gut feelings, relying on my own mind to save a marriage that was just not right. But the decision had finally been made and there was no going back, ever.

I fell in love for the first time when I was 14 years old. Oh boy, was he cute. Dark skin and thick black hair. His smile was enough to forget everything my mum taught me about boys. I was so young, but it was already complicated. I loved too much and ended up losing my first love. With a broken heart that would last for years to come, and the fear of ending up alone, I jumped into someone else's arms trying to forget that handsome boy I had loved so much and so deeply.

I ended up in a relationship that wasn't satisfying, while I was still longing for my first love. Why did I do it? Fear. Nothing other than the good old fear. I was so afraid no one would love me again, afraid of being rejected and abandoned that I ended up settling. Better to have somebody around, anybody really, than being alone for the rest of my life. Am I right?

I ignored all the signs, completely ignored the universe, and ended up married and a mum at the young age of 18 years old. I am a bit embarrassed to admit this, but I spent the next 20 years ignoring my intuition and pushing for things to work out. I prayed to God every night for several years "please help me save my marriage" in pure despair. Why couldn't I have a happy life and marriage? I had everything else, money, a career, a good car, a beautiful new house. "Please help me save my marriage" I pleaded night after night.

Something started to change within me around my fortieth birthday though. They say you change your perspective when you get to your forties, that you start looking at yourself and life in a different way. Well, I don't know if it was the dread of imagining myself as an old woman still trying to make a long-failed marriage work, or if it was divine providence, but my perspective did change.

Quite naturally, one night my prayer changed to "Please God help me, I just want to be happy".

And that was it. The universe listened to my heart felt prayer, and about a month later, I ended it.

It was hard in the beginning, I was in uncharted territory, I was completely clueless, I didn't even know how to get car insurance, never mind take care of all my other needs. So much to figure out, and feeling more alone than ever, how could I possibly make it through? But fear not, my savior was on his way to rescue me from loneliness and to take care of me. I didn't know how to do it by myself, so once he showed up in my life, I held on to him like as if he was the solution to all my problems.

Now, let's just take a break here. I always thought of myself as being quite successful and independent. It was a shock when I realized that I really wasn't. You tell yourself whatever you need to hear so that you can keep moving forward in life without having to face the real problems. You know what the real problems are, they come in the form of difficult questions that arise from time to time, which we completely ignore, thinking they are just stupid, and fearing we won't like the answers.

We all do it, right? At least at some point in life. "Why do I keep asking for help to save my marriage? What is wrong with it? How do I really feel about it?" These were all questions I managed to ignore for over 20 years. Eventually they caught up with me, like they always do. But at this point in my life, I was still blaming others for my misery, I was still angry, upset, sad and feeling nothing short of helpless. When Noah entered my life, it was like all my problems were solved and I didn't have to struggle any more.

Dark skin and thick black hair, just like my first love, he was charming, polite and available. I closed my eyes and jumped into his arms. It was beautiful in the beginning, we had so much in common and were eager to explore each other, emotionally, intellectually, spiritually and physically. I had been alone for 3 whole months and now I was completely in love and obsessed with a new man.

This time it seemed like the real deal, I wasn't settling, I really thought I had found my soul mate and so, I made him the star of my life and allowed myself to shine only when he was nearby.

Of course, it didn't end well. After just a few months we were no longer romantic partners, we were just friends and as far as he knew, I no longer had feelings for him. I had become so dependent of him that I could not afford to lose his friendship. He was captivating with a view of the world that completely resonated with me. I couldn't let that go too. He introduced me to the concepts of the Law of Attraction and shadow work and together we found a few more hidden gems. Everything about him was just right for me. So, for a couple of years, we explored these and many more concepts together, as friends. Only as friends.

And yes, my heart was still in his court the whole time, but I couldn't let him go. The same way I had believed I could not survive without a saviour, I also believed I would never be able to evolve spiritually without him, without our shared experiences and all his inputs.

This is where I was. I didn't know that I could love myself and therefore not need a saviour to make me feel worthy of love and happiness. That concept was totally strange to me. Self-love, what was that? My heart was broken, but I could see a light shinning far, far away at the end of the tunnel. As he went back into the dating life, my heart broke into even smaller pieces and I started reading all available books on self-love, anything that could help me heal or at least survive.

It's so interesting how the universe works. If things had worked out between us, I would've never found true love within myself. Yes, it was one of the most painful times of my life, but it was also more meaningful than any other as it made me look at myself.

In my book "A Journey to Self-Love" I explain all the methods I used to get myself out of the hole and slowly come back to life. I wrote that whole book thinking I had found true self-love and under the wrong impression that what I had found would stay with me forever. It was a big surprise when just a few months later I felt like the world was just having a laugh plunging me into absolute and complete despair again. Where is that love that I found, the love I wrote about, where did it go?

I felt like a complete fraud. How can I even sell a single copy of that book now that I knew it wasn't the real thing? But that is exactly how evolution takes place, one bread crumb after the other, at the exact right time, and when you are ready to understand.

You see, since then I came to realize that the Universe never shows you the bigger picture, instead it carefully shows you one single step at the time. It's like a trail of breadcrumbs, you follow one after the other until you get to a certain destination you never before thought was possible. Only then, can you look back and appreciate the whole journey.

Looking back, I can see how Noah played his part so well. I needed a crumb to get me away from my ex-husband. I was so weak and alone that going back to that failed marriage was a possibility, remote but a possibility. After I met Noah, I fell madly in love with him, like I never felt in over 20 years of marriage, there was no turning back now. He was instrumental on my letting go.

He also introduced me to my new path, a path to self-realization and self-love. But the crumbs started at the mind-blowing ins and outs of law of attraction, mantra chanting and breath work. At that moment in time, I found self-love. The kind of self-love I was capable of experiencing back then.

For me, that feeling in my heart was true love because it was stronger than anything I ever experienced before, it was the breadcrumb I so desperately needed to get to the next phase of evolution, the next step of my journey.

And this is where this book starts, right where the last one left off.

The Goddess

I was sitting on the back of the car on my way to London. I didn't feel particularly comfortable with the men sitting in the front, and I remember being grateful for having to sit in the back of that old car, thus avoiding hours of painful small talk. It was an old car, that smelled funny and was way to uncomfortable for my liking. But I valued my own space and was not in the mood for chit chat, so the back seat seemed like the best option. I didn't even had time for coffee that morning and the driver had no intention of stopping anytime soon. Why have I agreed to come to this meeting? I hate my job!

It was drizzling outside, a typical April morning and as I saw the drips hitting the window, I paid attention to my thoughts. I had monitored my thoughts many times before, on and off. I knew how our thoughts can influence our lives, but there was something different this time. What can I say, I was bored! With nothing better to do for the next 2 hours I decided to play a game with myself while the men chatted away about the price of diesel. I was going to pay complete attention to every thought, be it loud or subtle, I was on it.

I since found out this process is commonly known as "mental diet" and as the name diet implies, it was no fun at all. But it was very insightful, that I must admit.

That was the day when the breadcrumbs to my next phase in life started showing up. Somehow, I felt inspired to take on this practice and I can say that several years later it is still close to my heart. It evolved from a simple game of strained observation into a natural process that runs almost independently in the background of my mind.

What started as simple curiosity managed to open a can full of worms. Once I got the taste for it, I could not stop. How could I go back to that polluted mind of mine? No way, it was not happening, and so I kept on it, every single day after that.

Just a few days into this process and I could already feel the difference within myself. There were so many thoughts that were altogether counterproductive, the rampage of self-criticism and victimization kept jumping in to make a mess. I don't know what was more shocking, the number of negative thoughts or the fact that I had been completely oblivious to them until that moment. I was a complete mess. Feeling sorry for myself, trying to keep a straight face around Noah and crying myself to sleep every night. Where did all that self-love go? Why me?

I used my newfound practice of mental diet to keep me afloat. While I was monitoring my thoughts I didn't obsess about Noah, although I must admit that most of my thoughts at that time were about him. But I persevered with my practice, committed to make a difference and sort my mind out.

A few days later another inspiration came to me through a video of this law of attraction coach. It was a short video reminding women how amazing they were. You know, the sort of cheap motivational kind of videos I usually tend to dismiss. I like content, deep levels of information, superficial mainstream tacky videos are not usually my first choice. But for some reason I couldn't stop watching it. She mentioned the goddess within and kept saying I was the goddess of my own universe. For some inexplicable reason, at that moment in time, it made sense to me. I couldn't care less if it was a cheap motivational video, it spoke directly to me, so I listened.

I have always seen God as an outside masculine presence, I never thought about it this way, the Goddess within me, it just resonated. And she was a woman!

Yes, I did intellectually understand the concept of us all being one, part of the whole, but part of me continued to see God, now with the new name "Universe", as an outside masculine force.

We do live in a patriarchal society and many of us grow up thinking that God is a man with a grey beard, dressed in white, who sits somewhere in the clouds and causes havoc at the expense of innocent people. Although I believed in the concept that we all had a divine spark within us, the concept of a God that was somehow external to me still persevered. I kept looking for God, searching outside and no wonder I couldn't find Him. But this is a discussion for later, I want to go back to the story.

I couldn't shake that feeling of being an actual goddess, not just having a divine spark within me but of actually being divine. It was mind blowing and it made so much sense. It was like I was recalling a lost memory. I remember that same night, instead of the normal crying myself to sleep, I contemplated what it would feel like to be the goddess of my own universe. How would I feel, what would I think, how would I behave? I felt this calmness and peace inside of me and a certainty that I was safe and complete.

Things started changing for me very quickly after that night.

I started feeling very feminine over the next few days, which was absolutely out of character for me.

Yes, I am a woman, but I never felt feminine. I remember watching a video of myself a few years back and rewinding it a few times because what I was seeing did not match the idea I had of myself in my own mind. I was always a tomboy, not a pretty girl, and surely, I did not feel like a goddess. But for some reason the thought kept on coming and I started to learn how good it felt to be a woman.

I started contemplating every night before sleeping, what it would be like to be a goddess. I would just immerse myself in the feelings that were now becoming so familiar. I gradually felt more and more feminine. The way I saw myself start changing, I was becoming a confident and beautiful woman in charge of her own feelings and emotions. I felt sexy and even aroused simply by looking at myself in the mirror. Something was happening inside me; I could not explain what it was, but I was loving it. So, I kept playing with it.

These feelings continued increasing within me and I noticed several changes in my behavior. I started looking at myself in the mirror and really seeing myself, not just the body but my whole self. I would look at my eyes and feel deep love.

I started developing a relationship with myself, which up until that moment, was virtually nonexistant. I was falling in love with my true self, that divine being that we truly are. And it was beautiful.

Bubble baths become kind of a routine for me, self-care became more important, and I noticed it was easier to say no. If I didn't want to go somewhere or do something, I would honor myself and simply say no. No justification, no stories, no excuses. That felt liberating, definitely a breath of fresh air! I was becoming very confident, something I never had been in my whole life. I absolutely love to learn, self-improvement is one of the most important things for me (right alongside teaching - what is the point of having the knowledge if I'm not going to share it, right?), so with my new sense of self-worth, I plunged into the pursuit of knowledge. I read everything I could find about the goddess along with hours of videos on the subject. Anything touching the goddess subject, I studied. The goddess, that powerful archetype that lives inside us and that we can access at any point in our lives, independently of our gender.

I noticed how fed up I was of wanting and not having. I was fed up of feeling like my happiness resided in the condition of another human being loving me and wanting me. I felt like it was my turn to be happy, my time to be independent and strong and I was determined to fully embrace my feminine side.

I knew I was powerful, complete, perfect and worthy; I knew all that, I just couldn't remember the truthfulness behind those words. But I knew, deep inside I knew something was changing.

I found this guided meditation at one point where the archetypes of several goddesses were invoked progressively through the different chakras. It was very empowering and helped me embody those archetypes in a more consistent way. I started concentrating on the different attributes, the goddesses could bring into my life, from unconditional love to wisdom, compassion and self-empowerment. Every day I felt more in synch, more confident, more feminine, more alive. Getting my head around the goddesses was a difficult path for me to take. For me there was God and that was it. Looking at goddesses who had been part of mythology and getting cozy with them brought up some fear within me, like I was somehow breaking a rule. Again, we have been indoctrinated to think that pagan religions were wrong, and we could go to hell if we dabbled in them. But this really had nothing to do with religion, instead it had all to do with what already existed within my own being. Looking at the goddesses as archetypes helped me get over the fear and once that was done with, I kept digging for information and getting familiar with the feminine energy. And what a breath of fresh air.

After about three weeks since my trip to London, I noticed a certain disconnection between me and reality. It was like I was on a slightly different dimension from everybody else. I started withdrawing from most conversations. I completely understood that our thoughts create our experiences, and I was becoming frustrated with the fact that most people weren't ready to accept that, and rather preferred living in an illusory world. I knew I was the creator of my own life, that my thoughts were powerful tools, and so were everybody else's, but most of them didn't want to take responsibility for theirs.

I felt so far away from other people, there was barely anyone to talk to about what I was feeling, I was just out of place.

This was a feeling I experienced many times after this. When there is an expansion of consciousness, a spiritual awakening, we tend to withdraw from the world. The paradigm shifts and others can easily seem shallow and futile. This is a normal phase that should be honored. Giving ourselves time to readjust to the new reality is very important and beneficial.

The Ego's Death

The distance I felt between me and those around me continued increasing. I felt numb to the world, painfully exchanging pleasantries and occasional small talk with my work colleagues. But I kept doing my part, being as polite as possible and keeping my distance as much as I could.

Then on a Sunday afternoon I had the most horrible experience.

I felt like I was dying.

Out of the blue, I felt like I was going to dye, no physical symptoms, nothing that could justify what I was feeling, but I knew I was dying, it was really happening.

I was scared for a minute, I sure was. I had no control over what was happening, and I expected my lifeline to be disconnected at any moment.

I am not afraid of death. I have more than sufficient proof that life goes on after the death of the physical body, but in that moment, I felt like a part of my being was going to disappear forever, and it scared me.

I felt like something inside me wanted to hold on, wanted to survive, didn't want to go. After a few moments of breathing through it, I realized I was still there, but something had changed.

It was an unsettling experience.

During the following days, I tried to find answers for what had happened to me. I found the expression "ego death".

The death of the ego is not really a death as the ego is not a real entity. It's called the death of the ego because it's felt as an actual death. During an expansion of consciousness, sometimes there can be a temporary transcendence of the ego, so in the face of its own disappearance, the ego panics and tries to hold on, creating a terrifying feeling of impending death. Many spiritual seekers stop their journeys at this stage, the ego exerts too much fear that the seeker cannot push through and turns around, truly believing they will die. But if you have the courage to stick around and push through the fear, this experience can actually be a wonderful blessing.

The ego death happens in different stages with different experiences, but the first stage often happens after a spiritual awakening. There is an expansion of consciousness, the way we see ourselves changes, the way we see the world changes, which temporarily allows for the transcendence of our self-identity.

For a couple of days after this experience, my mind became very calm. It felt like part of my inner voice had gone quiet. I felt very confused about who I was, what was happening to me, but I had a sense of inner peace. Most of my thoughts had disappeared, and the ones that were left were very different from the habitual ones. All I wanted to do was go within, meditate, be still.

Three days after the original experience, it happened again. I was in a meeting with my boss, sitting across the table from her. I completely blanked her; it was as if she wasn't really in the room. I could see her lips moving and some sound on the background, but I had no idea what she was saying.

It wasn't as intense as before, but still lasted for a good few minutes. My boss kept talking, pointing at paperwork, and my body was responding like it was on auto pilot, but inside, I felt like I was dying all over again.

I felt completely lost as I couldn't find who I was. I can't explain it in any other way, I just did not recognize myself. I didn't feel scared, I just thought that I wasn't afraid of dying, so I completely surrendered to what was happening and it was over not long after.

My mind became even quieter than it was before, there was barely any noise. There was so much clarity. The day after the second episode, I had a curious dream.

I was standing right next to a well, and right in front of me there was this beautiful woman. She had long beautiful hair and an amazing positive energy. She was completely made out of water, flowing with a bluish hint, just like the surface of a lake kissed by a slight breeze. She spoke to me. Telling me she was my Divine Feminine, she asked me to look down.

I saw that she had no legs and following her body, I realized she was emanating from below my waistline; she was my own self. She said she had now space to awaken within me.

I felt like a different person at this point, the Maria I used to know was disappearing. I didn't know where this was all taking me, but I could sense in my heart it was just the beginning. I was incredibly grateful for what was happening, as disconcerting as it was, it felt like a marvelous gift.

All I wanted to do at this stage was meditate, I just wanted to be still. I started meditating several times a day, I would even sit in my car during my lunch break to have a quick 20min meditation.

Around 2 weeks after the ego death experiences, I was told off by one of my spiritual guides. Being a spiritual Medium, I often interacted with my guides and spiritual helpers, they were always very kind and understanding. This time it was different, he told me off quite abruptly, just like a teacher would assertively tell you to stop chatting in class, he said "Sit straight!".

It startled me; I was not expecting that at all. He then said, "How do you expect the energy to flow through you if your back is never straight?"

I didn't understand what the fuss was about, but it sounded important. So, from that moment on I started sitting straight.

The Awakening

Life kept going on, I slowly returned to some sort of normality. Interactions with other people became easier and meditation didn't seem to be as urgent as before. I was more relaxed although my practices were still a very important part of my day.

One day I went to visit my friend, the Shaman, whom I used to visit from time to time. Her sessions always seemed to bring me more clarity.

In that session, while in a light trance, I saw a white female snake tying my feet together.

When she let go of my feet, my physical legs remained lying on the bed as my spirit slowly rose up. I was completely disembodied from the waste down. It felt very strange. I was then placed inside the

circle of a Native American tribe. This tribe were the Shaman's guides, I always saw them when visiting her, they had a very powerful yet gentle energy.

While in the circle, I was invited into a spiral of white light where I was left floating midair, completely surrounded by white bright light with a slight hint of blue. After a few minutes I was brought back into the room. This was a very intense experience, and I was left with the energy pulsating within me for quite some time afterwards.

When I opened my eyes, the Shaman couldn't control her excitement.

With a huge smile on her face, she told me my Kundalini was going to be activated. I just stared at her with a blank expression, I didn't know what to say, so I didn't say anything. But I thought to myself that no way that was going to happen, Kundalini is very dangerous, I'm not interested. I didn't think she knew what she was talking about. Or so I thought.

Three days after my visit to the Shaman, five months after my trip to London, I was in a rush to get everything ready for my week abroad. I was very excited, my birthday was on the following day and I'd be flying over to see my family back in Portugal.

I went to visit my friend Noah to pick up my birthday present and we were able to squeeze a mind-blowing conversation before I left. We used to challenge each other, expanding our consciousness with every conversation. That day was no different, although a bit shorter than usual, I was already at home and in bed by 9.30pm.

I couldn't go to sleep straight away, I was too excited about my birthday, my trip, the conversation I just had. Instead, I decided to read an article about our own divinity and how connected we all are. I read that article a couple of weeks before, and really enjoyed the reading, so I gave it another go.

This time was different. I was in such a high that for some reason, as I read the words, I felt my consciousness expand, I felt every single word inside my heart, and I felt the connection with the whole world. I was the One in that moment. I felt so warm inside, so full of positive energy and I couldn't stop smiling as I laid down to sleep still in that heightened state.

That's when I heard the words in my head, so softly spoken that I almost missed them. "It's time to awaken your Kundalini".

I didn't pay attention, I thought it had something to do with what the Shaman had told me, so I dismissed it and went back to the feeling of oneness with the whole world, which felt amazing.

I was finally drifting off to sleep when I felt this tingling right in the centre of my back. I turned around but there was no one there, so, I turned back and closed my eyes ready to fall asleep again.

The tingling came back but now it was strong, and I now realized it was coming from inside my own body, not from outside as I first thought.

I observed it, not knowing very well what was happening, but the feeling was so good and positive that it could only mean it was a good experience.

Suddenly I felt an explosion of heat in the center of my spine that quickly went up burning everything along the way, my neck, even my brain. It felt like hot lava melting every bone and tissue in my body. It was somehow painful, but bearable.

Then I felt it on my feet, and the same burning sensation went up my whole body coming out the top of my head. It was a constant flow of hot lava burning my whole being from my toes to the top of my head.

I observed the whole process completely motionless and powerless. My body had been taken over by this mysterious energy, it was more powerful than anything I have ever experienced... and it was all coming from inside myself.

I couldn't move for what seemed to be just a few moments. It finally subsided and I reached to my phone to see the time, it was past midnight... I've been there for over 2 hours.

I tried to gather my thoughts but there weren't many. My mind seemed to have been wiped clean and I was alone in the dark, just waiting.

She came again, more intense than before and I could feel the movement of the energy going up and down my body, I could feel it burn around my spine as if a serpent was intertwined in between my vertebrae, squeezing me motionless.

I saw a couple of yoga positions in my mind's eye, but I couldn't get myself out of bed. Instead, I sat in lotus position feeling the energy take over me, take over my body, my mind. I surrendered to that powerful and loving energy that I felt could destroy every single cell within me if it so wished.

It eventually stopped and gave me some rest. It was 6:07am.

The Shaman was right after all.

At this point, I was exhausted but experiencing immense peace. All my thoughts were missing, in fact, through the whole process my mind had been completely blank, I was just observing and experiencing without narrative. All I knew was that my Kundalini had been awaken, so I closed my eyes and slept for about an hour before driving to the airport.

I was in a different world the whole day. Everything seemed different. I was different. As I hadn't seen my family in over a year, and it was my birthday, everyone was excited to see me, but conversations were strange and impossible to keep up with. I excused myself with friends and family, saying I was very tired as I had no sleep the night before, but honestly... I felt like I was an alien in a strange world and I could not wait to go into the quiet.

I couldn't have asked for a better birthday present.

My whole vacation was spent in a weird bubble. Every opportunity I had, I would excuse myself and either meditate or find information about what had happened to me. I spent hours researching and sitting still in the quiet.

Kundalini

This whole book is about my Kundalini awakening, I think it's time to explain what Kundalini actually is.

I first came across the word Kundalini many years ago, in an article related to spirituality. It listed all the problems the author had been through after his awakening, and how his life had been completely destroyed, not to mention the many physical ailments that had accompanied it.

The account was so terrifying that right there I thought the Kundalini energy was not to be played with, in fact I should stay away from it altogether. And so, I did. For years, I avoided everything with the name Kundalini, from meditations, music, to articles, books and videos. I wanted nothing to do with it.

Although a Kundalini awakening can in fact cause havoc in your life, it's definitely not something you want to stay away from. Let me explain this properly.

The word Kundalini means coiled in Sanskrit. It is believed that all humans have Creation energy coiled at the base of the spine. This energy represents the Divine Feminine and is often referred to as Kundalini, Goddess, Great Mother or Shakti.

It is believed that the One, All There Is, divided itself into two aspects: the Masculine and the Feminine. Shiva representing the Divine Masculine, consciousness itself, the unmanifested and the nothingness. And

Shakti, the Divine Feminine, life force, all that is manifested and the whole of everything. Together they are the One. In fact, the separation between these two forces is merely an illusion as the One is always the One, the separation is only perceived on this level of consciousness, in duality.

I will use the words Kundalini and Shakti interchangeably in this book. Although it is worth clarifying that Shakti is all that is manifested, and the Kundalini energy is therefore only one aspect of Shakti.

It is also worth noting that the energy is only Kundalini while it's coiled, becoming Shakti as it awakens and starts rising. Either way, for easier reference and understanding, I will use both words to express the same idea. This energy lies dormant at the base of every human being, coiled like a serpent. This is the reason the Kundalini is often represented by a serpent.

According to the masters and sages, this energy can only be awakened by the power of Grace, although it is said the touch of certain gurus can bring the energy to life. I have not experienced the touch of the guru, so I cannot elaborate on this. In my experience, Grace showed up a few days earlier while I was visiting the Shaman. The spiral of bright light that lifted me up leaving me buzzing with energy for hours is like many accounts of Kundalini awakenings. It usually manifests a few days or a couple of weeks prior to the awakening itself.

So, the Kundalini is the primordial Creation energy itself which is dormant. Once it is awakened it starts moving up the spine, through every energy centre, more commonly known as chakras. It will work on every chakra to clear blockages, illusions, karma and attachments so that an expansion of consciousness is possible and enlightenment, self-realization, can take place. This energy is very powerful, and it works not only internally, but also externally as it ripples out into every aspect of life. The more identified with the egoic mind you are, the more difficulties you will experience. The whole process is a purification of consciousness, where the illusions of being a person start dissolving and you can see yourself as part of the One, not as separate self with an ego.

For those who have no spiritual background or that are heavily identified with the egoic self, it can be a very difficult process to endure and resisting it can even cause physical pain.

When Shakti awakens, she does not stop until she purifies you completely and for that to happen, all that doesn't serve your expansion of consciousness will be removed from your experience.

Sometimes by force, other times you will feel like there is no other way and you just surrender.

Either way, from the ego's perspective, the losses are immense. You may lose friends, family members, romantic partners, jobs, careers, interests and finally you lose your own self.

No wonder most of the accounts you encounter on this energy are so dreadful, but only because we are looking at the whole process from the perspective of the ego. If you see it from the perspective of your own soul, then this is the best thing that could ever happen to you. You are finding your true self, finally seeing the illusions and transcending suffering.

Is it hard? It is very, very hard. But it has been the best experience of my life.

Back into life

As the days went by, I started feeling very emotional. It was like a lot of my insecurities were showing up, hitting me where it hurt the most. It took a few days, but I eventually understood that this was an opportunity for me to face those insecurities and fears, and so I did.

It wasn't pretty. I felt lost, emotional, abandoned, not important, betrayed, sad... and then I accepted all of it, I told myself I was God, I was the Essence, and all of these things were nothing but illusions. They weren't real. They were just shadows of a world that wasn't real any more. I could just let them be.

I realized that all the things I wanted had no meaning. I was complete within myself, and I lacked nothing or nobody. Shakti was showing me that life without suffering and full acceptance of myself was possible, the only real thing was the joy and the love within me.

It wasn't an easy process, there was a lot of suffering coming up for me, but I knew it was part of the process and an opportunity to remember who I really was. I felt very grateful for the whole experience, although some days were extremely difficult.

On top of the emotional disarray, I had many sleepless nights with the Kundalini energy burning her way up my body. The Kundalini is usually experienced when the body is resting or fully relaxed, mainly at night. But in the early days, she was active for the most part of the day and then again at night. My feet were constantly burning up and I could feel a lot of pressure in different parts of the body, as the energy was burning her way inside me.

I had occasional headaches, it felt like I was being burnt alive or like I was walking over hot coals, but I allowed her to have her way. Not that I had any control or power over her, Shakti is the energy of Creation itself, she goes where she wants to and fighting it would only make the experience more painful and hard. Instead, I learnt to relax into it and made myself available for this incredibly powerful energy. I completely accepted what was happening.

One night, the energy was particularly active and strong. It was the second night in a row where I had no sleep at all, just lying awake in bed as Shakti did her bit.

I felt it on the top of my head, on my Crown, then it came down to the Root on the base of the spine, followed by a rush up my spine. Then it moved around the Root for about half an hour. When it finished, I thought I could go to sleep, but she had other plans and came back shortly after to work on my Sacral. It stayed there for a long time, moving around inside my body at will, finding blockages, healing and dissolving.

Wave after wave, she came back to one energy center at the time. On some of them, the energy was more intense, on others it was just a light touch. She worked her way up until my whole body was touched by this spectacular energy. Last time I looked at the watch it was shortly after 4am. I had about one hour sleep before going to work.

On another occasion, I felt this rush of energy up my back when I was sitting at my desk at work. I just wanted to close my eyes and go with it, but I couldn't do that at work. There was so much energy pounding that by lunch time I had a massive headache, it felt as if the energy was trapped. I rushed to the car on my break and sat there for about 20 minutes, just resting in the quiet. It wasn't long until my Crown chakra opened up and I felt a release of energy. What a relief, in seconds my headache was gone.

Another time, the energy came as I was drifting off to sleep and concentrated on my legs. The energy was so intense, I felt my legs swell up, it felt like they were burning and had strong pins and needles. Even my toes were sore from the intense heat. It was like that for about two hours, once the energy cleared, I was able to have some sleep.

As the weeks went by, I started noticing how different I was. I was giving myself to the path, trusting and knowing that it was exactly what it should be, it was perfect. Of course, it wasn't comfortable, but nevertheless it was perfect. My mind was working in a very different way.

Throughout my life I had incredible encounters with angels, archangels, fairies, light orbs, Mother Earth's spirit, ghosts, power animals, mythological creatures and even an Egyptian god, but although all these experiences were absolutely amazing, and I felt honored with every contact, every conversation, every guidance and every word, this energy was different.

Up until this point, I could recognize the divinity in others and although I intellectually understood myself as being part of that same Essence and being divine in nature, I could not feel it. All contact was external, I was always looking outside.

The Kundalini is an inside job, it's the amazing creative power from which we are all part of, I could now recognize my own divinity. I was transitioning from the intellectual knowledge to a deep knowing within my heart that I was indeed One with everything.

Attachments

I always knew money and fame wouldn't bring me happiness, they're just excuses replacing what we're really looking for, which is our true self. Therefore, I didn't have many attachments to things or people. Or so I thought.

For a good few days, I could feel the Kundalini work on me, not only during periods of rest but throughout the day as well. It would cover my whole body, but only a couple of chakras at the time, and when they were all covered, the energy would start again from the beginning. I was sleepless and completely exhausted, but I was learning to allow the process and tried not to interfere.

One night, the energy came rushing and I felt a sharp pain piercing through the top of my mouth straight into my brain, and later connecting to my stomach.

I then saw my guide sitting on the edge of the bed looking at me. He told me that many changes were coming, I should rest both my body and my mind in preparation.

Well, I knew all this burning away, day and night, had a purpose, I could feel myself changing more and more, but I couldn't help feeling a bit apprehensive towards the future. All within was falling apart, would it now change outwards as well?

I tried to focus on the positives, after all I completely believed that my thoughts created my reality, and I wanted a good reality to manifest.

At this point I started having bursts of emotions coming up quite unexpectedly. I'd be doing something or talking to someone, and emotions would stir me up inside wanting to come out.

Sadness, fear, jealousy, anger. They would only last for a few seconds, not even allowing the time for tears to be formed. Nonetheless, the emotions would still manifest and be fully felt, I really had no choice in the matter.

It wasn't always easy being gentle with myself in the midst of those emotions. It was like I was completely out of control. But I wanted to accept what was happening. Only when we accept everything are we able to really love ourselves unconditionally, so I did my best to keep my chin up and accept without a fight. Although I could accept what was happening within me, life outside had become harder. Only three weeks earlier, I loved my job, but since the activation, my passion had disappeared, and going to work was becoming a struggle. The people, the actual work, the rules, the stories, the conversations, the unconsciousness of those around me, it was unbearable at times. But bills had to be paid, so I kept the show going feeling worse about it every single day.

I also started analyzing my relationship with Noah. We had been together romantically for a brief period of time, but I didn't seem to be able to let go now that we were simply friends. He was completely oblivious of my feelings for him, I didn't have the courage to voice them over fear of damaging our friendship. But I was starting to realize that what I saw in him was actually a reflection of myself, it had very little to do with him. Nevertheless, the attachment was still there, growing strong, and Shakti was on a mission to wipe out every single attachment I could possibly have.

Exactly one month after the activation, I could no longer escape, and the reality of my situation was clearly shown to me.

I woke up in the middle of night feeling very strongly about my life being a lie. I felt dishonest and a fraud. I had cold sweats, my heart was pounding, and I knew I couldn't live with myself this way any more.

My mind came up with excuses to how I would lose our friendship, that I was being silly, nothing had to change, that the feelings were my own and I didn't have to share them, but the feeling was undeniable. I was being dishonest with him, and I could not keep that up any longer.

I never felt so strongly about anything in my life, I knew that no matter what the consequences, I had to be true to myself. I compared it to those people who commit a crime and even if they can get away with it, they end up confessing as the consequences are a lot less painful than living with the guilt. That's how strongly I felt about speaking my truth.

There was nothing I could do right then at 2 in the morning, but I promised myself I would come clean at the first opportunity. It had to be done. The opportunity came up the next day, and it was in the perfect set up. While my mind was shouting loud and clear "don't do it, you will lose him forever", but I did not listen, and the words came out of my mouth. Just like that.

"I'm in love with you".

I cannot express the relief I felt. The feelings weren't mutual, but that didn't even seem to bother me much. I was at peace with myself, I had spoken my truth, no matter what the consequences.

After that, we slowly drifted apart and even the friendship died out.

This attachment was all wrong for me, it had been for a long time, but I had been so blind that I couldn't see it. Now, I could not unsee it.

This was the beginning of the destruction of all my attachments. This one was the most painful of all, but it gave me the strength and the wisdom to love myself, and the courage not to live my life in fear ever again.

A month earlier, when the Shaman told me what was about to happen, I didn't want it, I was even afraid of the word itself – Kundalini. Everything I had ever heard of Kundalini involved some kind of loss or physical pain. Every account described how going through it had destroyed relationships, businesses, complete lives, absolutely everything. I wanted nothing to do with it, of course. Who wants to lose everything, right?

I couldn't see the reality of this energy because I believed in other people's accounts and never took the time to investigate it for myself. Either way, with investigation or without it, I was now going through a storm, and it was a rough one. All those accounts seamed very real to me.

I had lost my closest friend, the person I was in love with, I couldn't relate to anyone, my situation at work started deteriorating and with redundancies on the horizon I was becoming very worried for my livelihood too.

Looking back today, I can't express how grateful I am for what the Kundalini did for me. Cutting that attachment out of my life was the best thing that could have happened. It taught me how to completely love and accept myself. It taught me how to be independent and love life again without the need for approval or attention from others. It taught me what love isn't about and showed me the patterns I had carried from my past. It taught me how important it was to speak my truth. Healing myself was a process that took many months, but it was also the biggest expansion I ever experienced.

When I started losing my attachments, I was in pain. Relief comes from non-attachment, but when you are still attached and unable to let go, it can become very painful.

One night, as I laid in bed, and felt the energy flow up my legs, I had a realization.

I realized that nothing outside myself would ever be able to make me happy. I read this in so many books previously, but having the understanding was something else.

I felt that even if I could get what I wanted, I would always be afraid of losing it. I would never be truly happy for longer than just a few moments for as long as I depended on outside conditions.

And just like that, I was free.

There was no need to chase any more.

The fear was taken away in a split second as I knew in my heart that the only one who can bring me long lasting happiness is myself. I am the only one who can truly and unconditionally love me.

Not the ego side of me that keeps shouting out loud how much I need things and people. The true me, the divine me whom I could sense every time I quiet my mind.

The true understanding of this fact was liberating, but it wasn't fully integrated at the time.

When we have realizations, they either have proper foundations to stay in place and forever change your paradigm or, as life starts happening, you will be slowly going back to old habits and beliefs.

Many have spiritual awakenings that are truly mind blowing, but somehow forget the whole experience months later.

As I am writing this book, three years after my Kundalini awakening, I refer to my personal journal where I wrote my thoughts and the daily occurrences as accurately as I could express them at the time. I do this so that I can explain my experiences correctly with virtually no deviation from what actually occurred. But as I read those pages, I realize I have forgotten so many of the experiences I had. Some of them changed my whole life, but they had been forgotten or resting on the back of my mind as a memory from a long time ago. The beauty in this process is that, even when you forget, the universe keeps bringing you new experiences and opportunities to remember. And once you had enough realizations, you just stop being whom you thought you were altogether.

The Heart

Approximately 2 months after the Kundalini activation, the energy changed. It was still manifesting on a daily basis, but instead of burning like hot lava all the time, it now felt like electricity. It was like having an electric current moving around in my body with the occasional hot lava burn.

One day, during meditation, I felt the energy moving around my body as usual, coming to a stop shortly after. As I was having some trouble quieting my mind, I decided to give up on the meditation for the time being. I still had a few minutes to spare, so I decided to browse for a little bit on social media, where I saw a picture of an old friend, I hadn't seen in over 20 years. That's when it happened.

I felt my heart open. It felt just like a flower opening slowly, one petal at the time.

I could feel a soft tingling caressing my heart centre as each petal opened.

Then I felt the Kundalini in my legs and watched as she rushed quickly through my body, exploding in my heart. My whole body was inundated with love, from head to toes I was tingling, and tears poured down my eyes. It was a beautiful experience. A love so intense, felt for the very first time.

The Heart Chakra, is located in the region of our physical heart, in the centre of the chest.

Every chakra is special in its own way, but the heart is a bit different from all the other ones, as it is the bridge between the lower and the higher chakras, or rather our physical aspects and our spiritual ones.

It's in the Heart chakra that we first encounter compassion and empathy. Before, we were too concerned with our survival, the way the world saw us and the way we saw ourselves, to even begin considering other people's feelings or wellbeing. But in the Heart, we enter higher realms of existence.

The Heart Chakra regulates compassion, empathy and unconditional love.

This is the centre where we can start transcending our ego's limitations and allowing new higher perspectives to be integrated. We start asking - how do I feel? Is this serving me? It's also the chakra where forgiveness and self-love become a possibility. It's the energy centre where our relationships can finally be free of wants and needs and we can love from a place that is pure and unconditional.

When this chakra is balanced you have meaningful relationships, you feel connected to the world outside and at the same time to your inner being. Although, if it becomes unbalanced, you can become co-dependent, feeling jealousy and needy. Or you may feel disconnected and start withdrawing from the world.

Now, the Heart chakra is not just about giving all our love, it's also about receiving. It encourages the balance between giving and receiving, in a way that serves everyone's greatest good.

When you experience love through the Heart chakra it becomes sweet and easy, it's not about romance and the reproductive instinct or lust, it becomes free of agendas and needs, allowing for free expression and acceptance of the self and others. It becomes free of conditions.

When we live life through the Heart chakra, the energy flows freely and we are able to see any situation without the need of judgement. We can begin to free ourselves and those around us.

Up until this point, Shakti had been working mainly on my lower chakras, the ones connecting me to the physical and egoic self. When there are blocks in the lower chakras, the Heart remains closed, except for moments when we experience great happiness or love. The toxicity of the lower chakras' blockages, the conditioning of the egoic self, prevent the Heart from opening, but when the lower chakras reach a certain level of purification the Heart no longer feels the need to protect itself and finally opens.

I started experiencing new levels of love from this moment onwards, a deep love and appreciation for life itself and everyone, like I had never experienced before. But although the Heart became open just over a month after the initial activation, there was still a lot of work to do before I could live entirely from the heart. It took almost 2 years for me to have the courage to completely surrender to the heart and let my life be guided in complete surrender.

Facing the shadow

After the opening of the Heart, I entered a completely new level of consciousness. I was taking the whole Kundalini awakening very seriously and I was ready to get my hands dirty if need be.

Life was being harsh; my mind wouldn't give me any rest and my emotions were out of control. I went through a phase where all I could do was cry. This lasted for days on end.

I cried in the car. I cried alone in bed at night and again in the morning. I cried in the bathroom at work. I tried not to show I was crying in the supermarket and at the gym. I couldn't stop crying.

Until a friend told me some very wise words: "remember, everything is an illusion".

Of course, it was, but I couldn't see it, I was way past the point of being able to see the reality of my condition. My suffering was completely self-imposed as I was allowing the egoic mind to take control of my thoughts and emotions, I was getting lost in the stories. It was all happening in my mind.

And just like that, it was all suddenly very clear to me. I finally understood suffering.

Again, I read all this stuff in books, I had all the intellectual knowledge, but I was missing the experience and understanding within me.

I realized that suffering is caused by the ego, all of it. Everything is, just is. Good or bad is just a matter of perception, the perception is the ego's input based on a lifetime of programming.

Then I thought that my whole life was nothing but a lie.

If everything we experience is created by our thoughts and feelings, and if mine had been controlled by the ego, which now I understood was not real in itself, then my whole life was a lie. I gave up my power to the ego and let it create my reality.

At this point, I had a vision. I saw Jesus being tempted in the desert, and I realized that the story is actually about Jesus overcoming the control of his own ego, he transcended it. Just like Buddha had to face Mara's temptations in order to become enlightened.

These were all references to the egoic mind, which can be very terrifying and even nasty when feeling threatened. I was threatening the ego's survival, so it was hitting me back very hard.

After this realization, my tears completely stopped. Shortly after, the Kundalini energy seemed to change again.

It wasn't showing up at night anymore and it was now manifesting as subtle waves of energy moving in different parts of the body.

It was stronger on my feet and Crown, but what I really liked was when the heart opened. It started happening dozens of times during the day at this point, I was living my life completely immersed in this love that kept pouring out of my heart. Suffering started looking very different to me, I could not unsee what I had seen, I knew it wasn't real, but an illusion of my mind, so it slowly started losing power over me. I can't say I was in complete bliss all the time, I was still working through my attachments and figuring out my illusions, but their hold wasn't as strong as before. I felt like I was somehow separate from the emotions that kept rising to the surface mostly unannounced.

One day, as I was being threatened by my ex-husband to spend the next 5 years in court fighting for my divorce, I felt the anger rise in me.

My throat closed, my heart started pounding and I felt the desperation take hold.

And then, what would have been completely impossible just a week ago, happened.

I realized that this situation was created by my ego, by my negative thoughts on the matter, he was only playing his part. I decided not to perpetuate the situation, not let circumstances dictate my state of being. None of it was real, only an illusion created by my fearful ego.

Having a completely clear mind at this point I just thought "it is not important, it isn't real".

In that moment I was able to let go, I was ready to accept the possibility of never, ever getting a divorce. That problem that was taking control of how I felt, a big harry monster holding me to ransom, lost all its power in a split second. I was happy either way.

And with this thought my heartbeat returned to normal and I relaxed. I felt happy, truly happy.

I would have not been able to let go of feelings like this just a few days before. I could see everything in a completely new way. I felt like I was becoming free. A couple of months later I was divorced. No fighting, no hassle, just a peaceful agreement.

This episode showed me how suffering was caused by myself to myself, there was nobody else to blame. All it took to resolve the situation was a change in my perception.

When our perception changes, everything changes.

Suffering had been there to show me I could see beyond the illusion and transcend it. I had been given an opportunity to remember the true essence of my being, the only truth beyond the illusions.

From this moment on, I stopped getting upset by what life was sending my way, I started seeing all situations as opportunities to see the truth. No bad, nor good situations, only blessings to help me remember who I was.

Contemplating

I got really intrigued, and wanted to understand what would happen when I'd become able to ignore the stories and illusions of the ego. What would happen to my life?

I started contemplating this for a few days in a row. I couldn't understand. If all my wants come from the ego what is the point in even living? Would there be any happiness at all as I would probably not even want to exist in the physical plane anymore? This contemplation got me really scared at one point. But then, I realized the fear I was feeling was just the ego fighting for its own survival. But nevertheless, the question remained, how will I even wish to create anything and have a meaningful life?

And then on my way home from work I had an aha moment. It was just a passing feeling with a sense of knowing.

I understood that once the ego had been discovered and could no longer control me, my wants and desires for experiences would come from my true self. They would still exist as they are part of life, the journey in remembering who we are, but there would be no attachments.

That's when true happiness in life starts, that's when life is created from the heart and not from the ego. That's when suffering is understood and transcended, and peace can fill our souls.

I really understood it and felt it inside my heart. I couldn't live it fully yet, but I had a knowing in my heart that it was going to be ok.

Perfection

I have always been a perfectionist, being born a Virgo, I strove for perfection my whole life. But the thing with perfection is that it limits you. I used to think my perfectionism was what kept me moving forward but instead, it was keeping me away from real experience and expansion.

I had to analyse everything, and make sure it was pristine before putting my work out there. Even a simple email at work could keep me stuck in a loop of self-doubt. Not to mention my own self, striving for perfection reminded me of all my imperfections, my mistakes, and shortcomings.

With the rise of the Kundalini, it became obvious that actual perfection is in the imperfections. All the processes I was going through showed me how messy life could become, how primal creative energy was when expressed, and the apparent chaos of it all. But behind the curtain I knew everything was of an absolute perfection. Every particle of my being was in the right place at the right time, everyone around me was living the perfect manifestation of themselves and the whole world was connected and moved in perfect harmony.

What was imperfect then?

Creation was perfect exactly as it was, so that must mean I was perfect too.

This was a very hard fact to understand, but the more I looked the more I realized that all my shortcomings were opportunities, all my mistakes were clues and road signs that kept showing me the way back to myself. How could they be imperfect? How could I be imperfect?

Like everything else, this realization came and made total sense, but from the moment of realization to the actual embodiment of the concept, it took time. It started with small things, I would do my best but not strive for perfection at work, then in little things around the house and eventually with my own self and others. I started accepting what was exactly as it was, without judgment or trying to change it.

From emotions to thoughts, from interactions to situations, gradually I became able to see everything's perfection. Our little minds fail to see the bigger picture, the lessons behind the so-called negative experiences, the opportunities for healing and growth, but they are there, all the time shouting for our attention. When we start embracing the world and accepting everything and everyone as it is, life becomes a wonderful work of art, you start seeing the magic all around.

Judgement eventually dissolves and pure acceptance and compassion takes its place.

My relationship with myself changed as I could now accept all parts of myself, even the ones I didn't like so much, everything was just perfect as it was. And with the acceptance came a sense of freedom and liberation.

We've all heard at some point that all we need to do to improve our lives is to love ourselves. It seems quite easy, but the truth is that most of my clients say they don't know what that means or how to do it. I will tell you the same thing I tell them, it all starts with acceptance.

Accepting our whole self, one bit at the time, not judging any part of what makes us the person that we are, be it thoughts, feelings or even our bodies. Showing compassion for our whole being like we would do for a small child, is where self-love really starts.

The more I accepted myself, the more I accepted others, the more my love became unconditional.

Thoughts

With time, my thought patterns changed.

Initially, I started noticing uncomfortable feelings, but when paying closer attention, I could see they were indeed very subtle thoughts. They were hiding, like nuances of what was supposed to be a full thought but were only fragments. I noticed them. I noticed every single one of them. They could not hide any longer, I could now see them approaching my mind almost as a thief in the night. They could no longer hide.

I would see them, acknowledge them, and let them go. No fight, no resistance, no arguments.

They had nothing to hold on to.

Although this phase lasted for quite some time, eventually life became a bit more chaotic, and it became more difficult to notice the more subtle thoughts. But there was an increased awareness and with time and practice I could sense tiny variations, both in my feelings and thoughts.

The smallest discomfort became unbearable, entertaining negative thoughts or feelings was virtually impossible as it was almost as if my body was being ripped apart. I compare it to a library. When you are out in the world everything is loud, from kids playing in the park, the birds singing, people chatting and cars passing by. You will hear all these noises but completely miss a whisper.

When you enter a library, even the whisper is loud, it can no longer be missed.

My mind became so quiet that whispers of negativity were picked up and dealt with immediately as if they had been slapped by the librarian's "Shhhhh!". Today, as I write this book, I still have negative thoughts, I still worry, I still get stressed. But the moment I do, it's evident that something is going on. I don't fight my thoughts anymore, I don't shush them or try to modify them as I used to. Instead, I accept them as they are, they are just thoughts after all, and there is nothing they can say that can hurt me in any way.

I simply changed my perspective from needing to change to accepting what is. The moment you accept a thought instead of fighting it, it starts losing power over you. But accepting the existence of a thought doesn't mean that you have to like it, entertain it or believe it. Very far from it. I accept the existence of my thoughts because I have no power over choosing them. But then, instead of engaging or believing them, I don't. Let the thought be, I'm paying attention to something else.

It's incredible how much energy you save when you stop believing your thoughts. You stop fighting what is being said in your mind and a sense of inner peace becomes apparent. Every time you fight a thought you are giving it attention, which means you are feeding it with energy and making it become more powerful. The moment you try to deny it or justify it, you show it that you are believing what the mind is saying, you are letting random thoughts which were chosen by the mind, control you. When you accept them as just thoughts that come and go during the day, you stop believing them and the need to engage gradually disappears. The thought loses its power over you and eventually dies off never to be experienced again.

Work

As time went by, I started having many realizations about myself, others, and the world. My perspective changed so much that it became impossible to see things the same way as I used to.

Conversations with people became either very deep or virtually non-existent. Small talk become too difficult; anything more than polite pleasantries was just impossible. I withdrew myself at work and little by little I realized how much it was misaligned with who I had now become.

A job that I once considered the best in the world, the job I had started just a couple of days after my separation, it had been my salvation in many ways, but it was now a nightmare.

As I have come to realize repeatedly, the universe will always bring you the experiences you need to make the difficult choices necessary for your continued evolution. Shakti was indeed on a mission to clear my path, in my inner world but also on the outside physical reality.

With the epidemic of Covid bringing the world to a standstill, I was lucky enough to work from home for a long period of time. Although it was a wonderful relief from having to commute for hours every day, it showed me how much the actual work was becoming a burden. It was not only the people around me as I thought, but it was also the work itself.

Over time my responsibilities changed slightly, and I become an instrument for the corporate world to exploit the little man. We were many in my department, but I was the one left with the horrible task of squeezing the very little profit small companies still had, to fill the pockets of those who had plenty. I became very conflicted and expressed my concerns many times but "orders are orders" was always the answer.

Until one day the universe pushed my limits to see how much I could take. The universe knows exactly what buttons to push and when to push them. I was unhappy for so long now but had no courage to take the leap until there was no other way.

I had to go in the office for a meeting with my boss, the department was changing and there was a whole new plan being presented. After a couple of hours into the meeting, with tasks now delegated and plans in place, the door opened unexpectedly and one of the directors came in. Without knocking or any other pleasantries, the message was simple and direct: "Stop what you're doing, the plan has now changed. We are deciding what you're going to be doing from now on".

I stood up like a spring being released, I was ready to walk away but looking around the room all I could see were my colleagues' look of confusion and the helplessness in my boss' eyes, so I sat down again and persevered.

At the end of the day, as I sat in my car ready to drive home, I was in a state of confusion and anger.

"Why is this happening?" I asked as I started a rant directed at my spirit guides. "How could you not tell me this was happening?", "Why?, Why?" The frustration was visible, and I was having a tantrum, of which I am not proud. Well, my guides did respond in a very simple way: "How much more do you need before you finally leave? What does your heart say?".

My rant stopped, my anger subsided and there was just this sense of clarity. That was my last day of work.

After this decision I felt so much relief, I was free, but a new problem was on the horizon. I had only enough savings to last me a couple of months and my side job as a Life Coach and Spiritual Medium wasn't going to make a difference.

My guides kept telling me almost every day that all I had to do was trust my heart, nothing else mattered, just what my heart said. At this point I was doing trance mediumship quite regularly and the insights I was receiving from spirit were a complete training program on how to follow the heart and surrender to the universe. All was under control, I was being looked after, even if I could not see it.

Month after month I trained myself to trust. Every time the worry and anxiety showed up, I acknowledge them and connected to my heart. The moment my money ran out was very worrying and all the trust I had been working on started crumbling. For a couple of days, I could not see a solution, and losing my home started to look like a real possibility. But I had a few sessions with clients, then added up some old savings I had forgotten I had kept in a drawer, and the money for the rent was miraculously there. Then something else showed up and little by little the money to cover all my bills magically appeared.

All my guides had to say was "keep trusting and follow your heart", and so I did. Month after month, the same routine happened. Always unexpected money from unexpected places, always enough for all my bills. As I'm writing these words, over a year has gone by and the same routine keeps happening, always unexpected, from different sources and always on time for all the bills. This was one of the biggest lessons I had to learn, the let go of trying to control everything and trust that my heart will guide me. The more I trusted the more I paid attention to my heart and started following its every demand and desire.

I became very sensitive to what the heart had to say, and always looked out for subtle contractions or expansions that indicated the direction I would be better off following. Every time I left the house I would stop and ask my heart what direction it wanted to go. When I listened and followed, every single time, I would have some kind of experience that was relevant for me at that time. From meeting new people and having engaged and surprising conversations, to meeting old colleagues I had forgotten existed but who were able to give me a new outlook into my past. Even billboards and car license plates were communicating with me, and I was starting to see magic in every corner.

The more I worked with my heart, the more that energy center opened, and I started seeing the world from the heart's perspective. I was putting my heart first, always, I was honouring my inner voice like never before. Loving and forgiving was becoming easier and there was virtually no judgement towards others or myself.

Eventually life started settling down and as my work evolved, a steadier income was now able to flow in my direction.

Trust in the Universe has become a natural thing for me, even when I get scared or cannot see the way out, I trust and allow magic to happen.

Suffering

One night as the Kundalini became active, I felt her rise from my toes to the crown in just a few minutes, to then rest in the 3rd Eye. With it came a vision.

I saw all the people in my life. It was a dark night, and it was raining. They were all in a group standing together.

Time stopped for a moment, it was not real anymore, everything just was, and I saw all of them completely naked. Not naked as without clothes, but naked as in I could see their true selves.

I saw their past experiences and their sufferings, and then it all disappeared. The suffering was not real, if time didn't exist then cause and effect did not exist either. I realized in that moment that what those people were showing me were just the stories I held for them, but stories are just stories.

Without past experiences their personalities couldn't exist, so all I was seeing was my own perception, the choices I made about those people. Without time they are, just are. They are timeless, infinite, and flawless. Just like me and you.

And without time, every moment is all that exists which means I can choose whatever I want in every now moment.

It's not easy to explain my two second experience in actual words, but in that moment, I understood that time is what keeps the illusion of reality together. Take time out of the equation and everything stops making sense.

The way I saw others changed drastically after this experience.

I never saw anyone as a victim ever again.

Sexuality

Being Creation itself, Kundalini is inevitably sexual energy. And although sexuality is still a tabu to many people, I will address it in this book as it is a huge part of the Kundalini process, and it played a very important role in my own awakening.

I was never a sexual person, having sex was never pleasurable to me, and during my marriage it became an obligation I often hid from. Yes, I was with the wrong person, but it was deeper than that. I had so much shame of my own body and orgasms seemed to be something other women were good at, not me.

Patriarchal culture was not a friend either, as I believed I had to please men, never the other way around. They wouldn't like me otherwise, I so often thought. I was frustrated for a long time and didn't even realize it.

After my Kundalini awakening, I started feeling a lot of sexual energy. The more I connected to my body and allowed the flow of energy run its course, the more sexual desire I felt and the more alive I become.

That is one of the beauties of Kundalini energy, she is life itself. The more you embody it, the more alive you feel. All my cells became alive, and I just wanted to dance and express myself. My creativity went through the roof, ideas started pouring for projects, books, collaborations, you name it. I even created a little book of ideas where I made notes almost daily of what I was intuitively receiving.

You see, sexual energy is not only confined to sexuality. Sexual energy is life's energy, it allows for creativity, intuition, self-expression, authenticity. I had been half asleep all my life but now I was fully awake.

Everything become pleasurable, I could see magic and love in every situation, in every animal and plant. I started understanding how I was connected to all of it, and how we were all so alive.

When Shakti reached the Third Eye Chakra this energy intensified. The energy had reached the brain, so, what was just an energy in the body until then, turned into a story for the mind and sexual thoughts became very predominant. They were mostly fantasies and desires, but in a way that it was almost impossible to turn off. The sexual energy was so strong that I could feel it vibrating in my body, feeling the rush of adrenaline running through my veins almost impossible to control. I can honestly say that I did lose control a couple of times, it was like Shakti herself was taking over my body and all I could do was observe what was happening.

One day I was feeling the rush of energy coming over me when the thought of an old friend, David, come to mind. We had a long history of mutual attraction, but conditions were never right in the past. As the thought of contacting him crossed my mind I fought it. I said to myself "that boat has sailed", "the timing is not right" and "no, I'm not going to contact him". As I finished this line of thought, I saw myself put the phone down. A message had already been sent and I had no control over it whatsoever.

I must admit that it frightened me a little to see that this energy was actually taking over my actions now. But it seemed like Shakti knew better than my little self and the time was now absolutely perfect.

Everything happened very fast. We became very intimate, very quickly. I didn't fight what was happening, for the first time I wasn't hiding myself.

The more I embodied Shakti, the more I felt like a goddess.

My shame and guilt had been healed and I was expressing myself in my fulness. There was no separation between me and Shakti anymore, we were one.

Turns out that all those preconceived ideas I had, about having to pleasure men and letting my own desires to one side, were not true. I allowed myself to be wanted and my body to be worshiped.

David was the perfect partner to share myself with, a kind and gentle man but with the strength, power and beauty of a Greek god.

In my work I often see people beat themselves up for having sexual desires. I see men and women closing themselves down to their own self-expression to only become increasingly frustrated. What most of them fail to realize is that the energy of life itself, the energy that brings them the love for life, creativity, and joy, is that same energy they are ashamed of embracing.

Sexual energy does not need to be expressed in a sexual context, but when there is an avoidance to do it, it indicates a blockage in the energy. And blockages of sexual energy won't just limit your capacity to orgasm, they will block life in all areas.

I had to face my own fears before I could be free. I had to look at those intense feelings of shame and guilt every time I explored my own body. But once I healed myself, my body became this source of not only pleasure, but of vitality and creativity. I unblocked all areas of my life and now Shakti was becoming more and more a part of my own being, no more holding back, just allowing the flow of life to take over.

At this time, I was also faced with another one of my old demons – attachment.

Things with David were very intense and as per my previous experiences, I wanted to fall in love and lose myself in that connection. But this time things were very different, I was different.

When the pull came to jump into it head first, I picked up on it and had the strength to pull back.

Old emotions came to the surface, trying to pull me into old behaviors and patterns, but this time it was all so different. I worked on my feelings and emotions, and it was all so clear, I was having an opportunity to let go of attachment, I was learning how to love without having to lose myself in the process.

This was something that I wouldn't have been able to do in the past, but now all conditions pointed to the new reality: I was free, I valued myself and I didn't need to be attached to someone in order to love them. And let me tell you that when love happens without the attachment, there is no agenda, no needs or wants, there is just an appreciation of the moment, of what is.

Shakti was so right, it was indeed the right time for David and me, it was the right time for me to learn this lesson and David was the perfect teacher. For that, I will be eternally grateful.

The Crown

Since the rising of the Kundalini to the 3rd Eye Chakra, I had noticed a change in my spiritual journey. I had been concentrating so hard for the past 3 years to heal all parts of myself, diving deep into shadow work and facing all my demons, but something changed at that point, and I felt lost.

It wasn't just the increase of the sexual energy, it was more than that, I felt frustrated with all of it.

Although I was walking the path of the goddess, the Divine Feminine, my approach to enlightenment had become very masculine. I was approaching God in a very mental way, learning as much information as possible, analyzing everything and trying to find ways to reach the goal -enlightenment.

I wanted it so much and had worked so hard for it that I started becoming frustrated for not being able to achieve it. Don't get me wrong, I knew the theory of it all, enlightenment is not something you achieve, it is something you already are. But the desire burnt very deep, and it was very much alive in my mind.

Six weeks after reaching the 3rd Eye Chakra, Shakti was now at the Crown.

Following an hour-long conversation with a friend who was excitingly telling me all about his recent energetic expansion, I felt immensely inspired. I did some work, wrote a few lines with powerful messages but was forced to stop shortly after by the energy that was coming over me.

My Crown Chakra opened, and I could see a white bright light coming down my central channel.

Although very strong, the energy had a sense of peace and calmness to it. It wasn't the same energy as the Kundalini, this one was coming from above and the whole feeling was very different from what I was accustomed.

Having my Crown open while the Kundalini was active was very common for me, except that the energy always stopped at the Crown. This time, the energy was coming all the way down through my Chakras until it reached the Root. A few moments later, it proceeded all the way down to my toes.

I could see my Sacral, Heart and Crown Chakras light up and connect with each other.

At this point the energy felt more like wisdom, an inner knowing and truth. This is difficult to express in words, but it had a feeling of sacredness and purity to it. It was sensed as being Masculine energy, equally strong as the Feminine, but with a completely different feel. I'm going to call this energy Shiva – the Hindu god of destruction that symbolises pure consciousness. In the Hindu tradition, when Shakti, the goddess of Creation is ready, she rises to the Crown where Shiva, pure consciousness, is eager to receive her. Shiva can then join Shakti in the body and when the body is purified, they can finally rest together in the Heart. Their union is often called the sacred marriage of Shiva and Shakti and represents the balance of both Divine Feminine and Masculine energies, but also the union of creation and consciousness. Shiva remained in my Root as Shakti Kundalini came on-line. She proceeded slowly up the Chakras and once she reached the Crown, I felt both energies intertwine over the Root and Sacral chakras, it was like they had become one energy.

I could feel Shakti trying to pierce the Crown. Almost like there was an invisible barrier that she was hammering on, trying to break through, unsuccessfully.

This lasted for almost 2 hours.

The next day, I was again forced to stop what I was doing and sit down in meditation as the Kundalini was becoming stronger. She went all the way up the spine and a few minutes later Shiva made his presence known and came down all the way down to the Root. I felt pain in most of the Chakras as he was slowly working his way down.

For a few minutes I had one side of my body burning and going upwards while the other side was cooler and going down. It was a very weird sensation, I literally felt like I was divided in two. My mind kept going blank throughout this process.

I was very curious about what was going on, so I asked Shakti if she was still on the 3rd Eye Chakra as I could not understand what was happening. As I asked this question in my mind, I felt a rush of energy shooting up from my toes upwards, passing every single energy center on her way up. When it reached the Crown, I felt like my bone marrow was being pulled upwards, I could feel my neck and my head getting straighter and taller. Shakti had pierced the Crown. This lasted for a while, I could feel both energies, Shiva and Shakti, working on me.

Two days later, the whole process evolved into a whole other level.

As I sat down to meditate and observe both Shiva and Shakti working, I was shown a series of hand mudras, which I tried to recreate as best as possible. I was also prompted to open my solar plexus and let all the toxicity out. I saw black paste like energy coming out until it was all gone. After this, I saw both strands of energy intertwine on the Solar Plexus. The lower chakras were already connected from the previous session. There was also some toxicity on the throat that I cleared and after that, the energies intertwined all the way up pass the Crown. It looked like a DNA spiral.

I felt like I was in a light trance during this whole session.

It became very scary when I stopped breathing. I wasn't able to control it, the breath just stopped altogether for a few minutes. I then felt like my consciousness had moved from my head to my whole body. It was like my whole body was consciousness itself.

Then I felt a pull, like my consciousness was being stretched, not just within my room, it was being stretched all the way to the other side of the world and eventually into outer space. The same repeated for the other side of my body, I was stretched beyond limits. It was then time for my consciousness to be stretched from the top of my head, I felt the pull, but it didn't just pull upwards, it joined with the sides, and it expanded all around, my consciousness was now everywhere.

I saw a hummingbird on the other side of the world flapping its wings in slow motion, then I saw a drop of water in the ocean followed by a spec of dust in outer space. I could see everything; I was connected to everything.

My Heart came into play straight after, it was time to expand it too. But instead of expanding in stages, it ripped wide open all the way out, as wide as the consciousness, in less than 1 second. I felt a sharp pain through the heart. I then saw all the hearts in the world, beating inside my consciousness and my own heart.

The immensity of it all was overwhelming and I could not but feel a degree of fear, I was afraid I might hurt others if my mind wondered with the wrong thought.

My mind wondered into the void where there are no thoughts. I kept surrendering and stayed in a light trance for quite a long time.

Trust Shakti. Shakti knows

With the rising of Shakti, a new set of old emotions started coming up. I noticed old patterns showing up from old relationships, and now I was looking at them in a completely different way.

Sure, the mind was still trying to bring me into the habitual feelings and reactions, but there was a part of myself that no longer identified with any of it.

I became more detached from certain people. The drama didn't seem to affect me as much anymore. I learnt how to step back into the wiser part of my being and let it speak for me. It didn't mean that I didn't care anymore, it just meant that it couldn't really affect me as it used to.

But there is always an exception, and my biggest lessons have always been on the realms of relationships. My perspective was changing, and I was not seeing my relationship the same way as before, it seemed to be getting a lot deeper and more connected. This, of course, brought my insecurities back to the surface. I could feel myself falling in love and with those feelings, a fear of losing my beloved started haunting me. Not that there was any indication of such possibility, but my heart was afraid of getting hurt again. My previous relationships had left me in such a horrible state, and I was afraid it could happen again.

There was a difference though, this time I could see what was happening. I could see my Root chakra kicking in with its need to keep me safe and secure. I couldn't ignore the emotions, but I could see why they were coming up. It was time to heal them, once and for all.

I embarked on a mission to heal those parts of myself, but it wasn't working. Nothing seemed to alleviate my fears and insecurities. So, I asked for help, I didn't know what else to do and I was afraid I would soon start sabotaging my relationship. I asked for help and of course, like always, it came shortly after.

I had a few realizations within the span of a few hours.

First, I realized that the Root Chakra's function is to keep me safe and secure, which meant that it will never stop trying to do so. Those thoughts and fears will always come up, no matter how much I try to heal them. I did so much healing that I didn't really think there was anything left to heal in that specific area. I realized that all I had to do was accept that those safety and security thoughts will always show up for me, I just don't need to accept them as being real.

Secondly, a few hours later, I realized that I was trying to build the whole house while foundations were still being set. I was still going through an awakening. Every spiritual or Kundalini awakening follows a certain process, that we can't really escape from. It starts by destroying everything that doesn't serve us, burns bridges, alienates people, blows up any sense of security, irradicates your sense of self before it can start rebuilding on strong foundations.

I was shown that I wanted the whole relationship to be set in stone so I could feel secure, so that my heart could feel safe, but the foundations were not yet finished. I was being destroyed for the past 3 years, and I had literally just been through a major change, how could I expect life to settle down if I wasn't out of the roller coaster yet? This realization brought me a lot of peace. I actually felt sorry for David, I thought that on an energetic level he must have felt he was dating a completely new person. All I had to do was trust.

After this, I heard – "Trust Shakti. Shakti knows."

I was trying to trust the universe was going to look after me, but there was a contraction every time I thought I had to leave it to the Universe. But when I heard these words, I was taken back to review the past 3 years.

I saw how Shakti's first mission was to have me speak my truth to the person I had been in love with for so long. I had been stuck in that toxic relationship for far too long, it had to end. And although it was hard, very hard at times, looking back it was the best thing that could have happened to me. It allowed me to become me. Shakti was looking after me in ways I could not comprehend at the time.

But she was, and it worked out so well.

After that, every time I trusted her, she always delivered. She always looked after me, in a way that served my spiritual journey and my greatest good. Not the petty desires of my little self, but the urges of my own soul.

I was able to trust her and leave a job I hated. I was able to trust her when there was no money coming in, still it materialized from the most unexpected places, and I was able to pay my rent every single month. I was able to trust her, and the wrong people left my life while the right ones came closer.

Looking back, I could see how much she had done for me, and I could not but feel gratitude. And just like magic, the contraction I felt when I thought I had to trust, became a knowing that trusting Shakti was the only thing I could do. Trusting her was the only thing that was ultimately going to keep me safe and secure. And so, a new level of trust and inner knowing was born.

I trust Shakti. Shakti indeed knows.

Kali

Approximately 3 weeks after Shakti reached the Crown chakra, I had an encounter with the goddess Kali.

Kali is the Hindu goddess of death and destruction. She is one of the embodiments of Shakti, and although she is considered fierce and ruthless, she is also capable of great love. As a dark goddess, she is greatly misunderstood. The ego will fear her greatly as she has the capacity to slay it and destroy everything that does not serve your soul's higher good. And the reason why she's called dark it's because she travels deep into the shadow to unearth everything that needs to be healed and released.

I first encountered Kali about a year before, shortly before I left my job. There was only a rush of energy accompanied by the name Kali, and I knew right away I wasn't going to like what was coming for me. I struggled, I fought it, but in the end, it was the best thing that could possibly have happened.

With time, I developed an admiration for Kali and a strong reverence.

This time, my encounter was very different. I sat in meditation feeling my Crown open as a rush of energy came all the way down my body. I heard a noise in the room and opened my eyes to see what the source was but couldn't find any. Instead, I watched with great surprise the fact that I had grown arms. I had now 6 arms coming out of my body. Two joining hands at the top of my head, two more opened to the sides with palms up, and finally my own arms, resting below my belly button.

This was odd but I was curious and wanted to know what this was all about. As I closed back my eyes to go within, I saw Kali right in front of me. Black hair and dark blue skin, the goddess was looking directly at me. Her arms were on the same positions as mine were just a moment ago, and her pointy red tongue was sticking out. There were no words. I knew exactly who she was, no introductions were needed.

I noticed she was holding a dagger with one of her many hands, and as she walked up to me, I actually feared for my life. I was motionless, sitting in lotus position just observing her movements. She came closer to me and used the handle of her dagger to hammer the floor between us. She hammered it once, twice, three times as it finally gave in, and pieces started falling out. It looked like quicksand, brick by brick disappearing in front of me into the abyss. I can now understand something I heard about Kali a long time ago – "she will leave you no floor to stand on". That's exactly what she was doing to me.

She stared into my eyes, and although there were no words, I knew she wanted me to look at her, to focus on her instead of what was happening around me.

She kept staring me in the eye, as the floor was slowly disappearing below. I knew I could trust her; I knew she was there to slay some part of me that did not serve me any longer. Despite the fear my ego was feeling, I surrendered to her and opened my arms telling her I was ready to die by her hands. Everything seemed to disappear, and I was back in my room.

I must admit that I was shaking at this point, I knew she was there to help me in some way, but I was very scared for my own survival, or rather my ego was scared it wouldn't survive to see another day.

I had only a few minutes until my Crown opened again, there was so much energy pouring in that I was forced to close my eyes again.

As I turned within, I could see Kali was still there, still in front of me staring me in the eye as the floor kept being stripped away.

Her whole appearance changed right in front of me, she grew taller, her feet and hands turned bigger with enormous claws, and a pair of wings grew on her back. At this point she also lost her feminine look and started to resemble more like an animal.

She took a step forward stamping her foot so hard that the remainder of the floor fell away. As this was happening and I started falling, she grabbed me with one hand and flew upwards. With one quick movement, using what seemed to be all of her strength, she threw me in to the hole, like I was some sort of basketball going through the hoop at the last second of the game.

I felt myself fall into nothingness for quite some time. The speed seemed to be increasing as I pierced what felt like an invisible barrier. I was going through what seamed another world but although I could not see or feel anything, I had just a sense that it was some kind of hellish place I would not want to be stuck in. This was right in the middle of the Earth, and midway through it, I realized I was no longer falling down but rather upwards. I passed the invisible barrier again on my way out of that place, and continued the upward free fall until I emerged on the surface through another hole.

I wasn't hurt, I had a bit of a bumpy ride, but I was ok. so I stood up and looked around at my surroundings. It was filled with light, blue sky and green grass. Flowers were everywhere and all the colors were so bright and diverse. I was alone for a couple of minutes until Kali appeared next to me.

I was very surprised to see her features had changed so much. She looked like the most beautiful woman, long black hair falling down her back, her skin was now of a lighter blue and everything about her was kind and soft. She held my hand and took me to a water spring nearby. As I sat on a rock, she gave me some water from the pure sparkly spring, and I noticed I had flowers around my neck. I was not expecting to see that my skin had changed color too, it was now a very light blue.

I felt completely at peace, but it wasn't long until Kali brought me back to the present moment.

There I was again, standing on the floor that was crumbling with the fierce Kali staring into my eyes.

She made me feel like it was time to really focus on her and ignore everything else around me. As she leaned forward and stared even more deeply into my eyes, I heard the words "It's about to start.

I will be quick".

And I was back in my room again.

The following 24 hours were very stressful. Suffering in anticipation can be horrible, especially if you do not understand what is going on or what to expect. I entered a mini phase of self-pity, feeling sorry for my little self who was going to go through some proper difficulties. I did not beat myself up for feeling that way, I literally felt like I was going to be killed and die a horrible death. I had met Kali before, and I knew it was not going to be pretty. Of course, this was the ego's fear, maybe fear of obliteration, which is one of the best gifts Kali can bring to those on the self-realization path as I was.

So, after a walk in the park to clear my head, I realized how lucky I was.

Shakti was taking me on the most amazing journey towards the remembrance of my true self. Shiva, the literal Grace of God, had descended over me and was offering me nothing but Love. And now Kali, was taking her time to set me free. Not to mention my beautiful guides and spiritual helpers that have been with me through this entire adventure. The gratitude in my heart just grew and expanded and I knew it was time to own my journey. I knew I had to trust the process, this was my journey, and I was not a victim of it. My Soul had chosen this path, so I was going to honor it wholeheartedly.

I'd love to be able to say that Kali's visitation had been just my imagination and that nothing had come out of it. This was not the case.

The days following Kali's initial visit I started worrying about what was going to happen. I was hoping it would be nothing more than an internal process, possibly involving some crying and releasing of emotions. Again, this was not the case.

About a week later, Kali showed up again. I was in my room when I saw her standing by the door.

She looked me in the eye but remained silent the whole time. Kali actually seemed serene, not at all threatening, which was somehow comforting. I looked at her and told her I was ready, "let's get this done with". With these words, Kali disappeared.

The following day started peacefully, nothing much to point out. I meditated for about an hour, had a shower and breakfast. All seemed pretty normal, but unexpectedly a discussion came about between my son and I. I will not go into the details of our discussion as it is not relevant to this book, but all I can say was that it was greatly out of proportion.

It was quick, but words were said that were impossible to take back and before we knew it, we were parting ways. The whole discussion was surreal, like I was watching two actors playing a part in a movie. I was aware of what was being said, but I didn't seem to be in control of what was being vocalized. I had this feeling that I previously knew the script and was now just acting it out. Just like the text message I had seen being sent to David a few months before by a force that I could not control, so was now a role being played that seemed to have its own will. In just a few minutes, the discussion was over, and life would never be the same. I thought of Kali, I knew this was only the start of her work. Surprisingly, I was ok. I was relieved and grateful as I knew this separation was needed, for the sake of both of us. I thanked Kali and braced for the next impact.

Energy

When I was growing up, I used to see people's energy. I didn't know what it was at the time, and I thought everyone else could see it too, but it turned out it wasn't so. The first time I mentioned what I was seeing to my family was also the last one, as it was taken as fantasy and make believe. I was told to stop being silly.

I slowly shut down that gift deeming it as just a daydream.

But up until that day, I could see people's energy. I could see how it expanded or contracted in different situations. I could see different people's energies dancing together in different patterns and I could even see how the energies behave when people said their goodbyes and went their separate ways.

It wasn't just colors; it was like the energy was alive and moving based on its "owner's" behaviors and internal state.

Sometimes, when I was on my way to school holding hands with my sister, I would briefly let go of her hand to see the energy retract momentarily before coming back to its dance when our hands found their way back to each other.

Since this gift was shut down, I rarely thought of it, it belonged in the past, although when doing healing or other energy work I could still see the energy. But it was different, it was only when healing was being performed, not at all like the wonder of seeing energy patterns dancing around people and the world.

With the rise of the Kundalini this gift came back online for me. I started seeing the movement of the energy again, and I could even sense how the energy was behaving towards situations and other people just by hearing someone speak.

As time went by, I started seeing the whole world on an energetic level. Of course, I could see people and the world as I always did, in the conventional way, but I could also sense the energetics behind everything, and a lot of the times, I could also see it. At this point, a lot of my conversations started with "you know I see everything as energy, so...", as facts weren't relevant at all, only the energetics started making sense to me. You'd be surprised to see how many people say one thing while their energy says something completely different.

Life had been magical all along, I just had shut it off so the world seemed as normal as it could be, but it wasn't. The world is connected, people, animals, even the trees, the ocean, and the elements, all of it is part of this marvelous dance of which we see only a glimpse of.

The more aware I become, the more I could see the connectedness of all and how a simple thought can greatly influence the collective. It's like the whole world is constantly speaking, and we have the chance to listen and understand, if we are willing to open up to the magic. With this new perception, I started realizing how perfect everything really is. Me, everyone else, every situation, the world, absolutely everything is perfect.

I started noticing a difficulty in maintaining conversations with people as most of us see the world as a place that could be great if it wasn't for this or that. I was embracing my authenticity, my own true voice and entertaining conversations that were so obviously just illusions, was extremely hard for me.

And as most of my conversations were being directed to a spiritual and holistic view of the world, I ended up always giving my honest opinion – "You know I see everything as energy" was almost as a disclaimer for what I was about to say but did not seem to be a good enough excuse for some of those outraged by my comments.

I must admit that the so called spiritual people were the most difficult ones for me to relate to. The spiritual ego can keep you thinking you know everything and prevent you from considering other points of view. You would expect open minds and hearts, instead I encountered, time and time again, the usual "of course God is perfect, but still those people should not exist" or "you can't tell me the war is perfect and just expect me to agree with you".

The truth is that for me, it doesn't matter what it is, it is perfect.

We might not like it, we might not understand or comprehend it, but it doesn't mean it is not perfect. I was still having a few tantrums now and again, whenever my little self felt threatened or insecure, a lot was happening in my life that was challenging and difficult to endure, but I could see the perfection of everything.

I could see how the past was horrible to my little self, but how my soul was beyond happy to have gone through all of it. I could see pieces of the puzzle fitting together like never before, still it was difficult to express it.

How could I tell my friend who had just been left at the altar on her perfect wedding day, that her experience was so incredibly perfect? How could I not sound horrible if I had said anything else but "my heart goes out to you". But still, I knew that was perfect, the whole situation had to happen exactly as it did.

I became fully conscious of this new way of seeing the world one morning as I sat in meditation. I had been doing some work with the archetypal energies and I had come into the habit of saying "I'm ready, show me what to do next" or "show me the way forward". On that morning, as I closed my eyes, and my mind vocalized the now familiar "Show me..." I stopped mid-phrase. In that moment I realized there was nothing to be shown, nothing to do, nothing to change, nothing to achieve, everything was so perfect right there and then. My mind went quiet, and I sat in the perfection of that silent moment. I knew everything was perfect.

As I confided with my father one afternoon about the way I was now seeing the world, I did not expect to hear what he was about to say: "you're becoming enlightened".

I cannot express how happy my ego was to hear those words. An immediate "I'm achieving it, I am about to do it" jumped straight into my mind in complete excitement. As I noticed that internal reaction, I saw how childish and ridiculous the whole thing was. The ego was happy it was achieving a state it could never achieve, and was all the way hoping for perfection to arrive while negating it in the present moment.

But what is this enlightenment we hear about?

Enlightenment

I was 15 years old when I first saw the movie "Little Buddha" starring Keanu Reeves. The movie touched me in a very profound way, and little did I know it had planted a seed in my heart that would stay with me to this day.

The movie touches upon Buddha's life, revealing his journey to enlightenment through his many ordeals and realizations. It was fascinating and I left the cinema theater thinking that my mission in life was to become enlightened.

I didn't understand what it actually meant, I couldn't grasp the work that needed doing, I understood absolutely nothing about it, I just knew that was my destiny. I knew it in my heart, in my gut, I knew it with my whole being.

Even when life become busy and difficult, whether I was struggling or content, my spiritual journey was always on the back of my mind. The desire to become enlightened, to overcome all my humanness and achieve the sought spiritual climax was my ultimate goal.

Deep inside I didn't think it would ever be possible. I couldn't just leave everything behind and sit in a cave somewhere or join an ashram in India. It was all I wanted but mostly an impossible dream. I had little or no hope of achieving it, but my heart never let me forget it.

After my Kundalini activation, I went on a mission to find as much as I could about this energy and what it all meant. I was surprised and beyond happy to discover that the final stage of the Kundalini activation is enlightenment itself. Once the goddess awakens, she will go all the way, but it can take a moment, a decade or even a few lifetimes. There were no assurances that I would achieve it in this lifetime, but it seemed all the sages agreed, this would eventually be happening for me.

But what is enlightenment after all? Here I am talking about a goal, something to look and work for, but what is it really?

Let me start by saying that all you ever heard about enlightenment is probably wrong, and you should leave all your pre-conceived ideas to one side before reading the next few paragraphs. Contrarily to what I always thought, enlightenment is not something you can work for or achieve. It is not something that happens to you, that will change you or take away all your humanness or your problems. Enlightenment is our unaltered state of consciousness, it's who we already are and there is nothing we can do that can bring us that experience, because it's not an experience.

The ego is the part of us that wants to achieve it, work towards it. The ego wants it so bad that will keep you seeking for it your whole life. And the ego is the one who will never realize it as the realization of the true self immediately implies the non-presence of the egoic mind. The enlightenment the ego so much desires, will never be achieved by the ego as it symbolizes its own death or transcendence.

I know this is a little difficult to wrap your mind around but bear with me for a second and I will do my best to explain it. As Rupert Spira once said:

"There is nothing exotic or mystical about enlightenment. It is simply the recognition of something that was always known, indeed is always known, before it is clouded by experience."

Or like the Zen proverb so perfectly puts it:

"Before enlightenment chop wood carry water, after enlightenment chop wood carry water"

Enlightenment is simply the realization of your true self beyond the illusions of the egoic mind. We are all already enlightened, it's our natural state, but we have been so conditioned by the mind and all our life experiences, that we have forgotten our essence.

In the end, even the desire to become enlightened needs to be surrendered as the only one who truly can desire it is the egoic mind. Your true self has no need to achieve it because it is already it.

With this I'm not saying that you should give up all your spiritual practices and just rest in the knowing that you are the Essence itself and therefore self-realized. Although you are, for you to really understand this, you will have to do some work in purifying the little self to a point where it can start accepting such concepts and even recognizing its truthfulness in the day-to-day life. This understanding should not be an excuse to not work on yourself, after all, you are still living a human life and you are still being conditioned and very much controlled by the egoic mind. It takes time to purify the lower mind and start elevating it to understand and even experience such concepts.

Although no work is ultimately needed, there is indeed work to be done until your true nature becomes something you know and not just some intellectual concept.

With the Kundalini activation, my lifelong desire became for the first time a possibility, but the closer I approached it, the more I understood it was not what I thought it was. The realization that my true self is always here, it is not something that I lost and now I have to find, it has been here, always, I just didn't know it. So, I was all the time seeking for liberation without understanding I had been free all along.

Self-Identification

Of course, until all these realizations become abiding, we go backwards and forwards in our understanding of ourselves and the world.

As my exploration continued, I started looking at my self-identification.

I had done so much work with my thoughts, there was so much awareness over the stories and habitual patterns, but I felt there was a piece missing. It wasn't just the movement of the mind that was keeping me in the loop of identification, it was deeper than that. Otherwise, I would abide in self-realization just by quieting the mind. And, let me assure you, my experience was in no way abiding.

As I investigated what was keeping me in the loop, I realized there was a sense of ownership behind the thoughts. Yes, I'd seen it before, but I was always under the impression it was washed away as my awareness increased and as I gradually stopped believing the stories my ego was telling me. One night as I laid in bed, I noticed a thought rising that was uncomfortable. My mind contemplated the possibility of something I wanted not coming into fruition. I felt the familiar contraction, sadness and anxiety that usually accompany this kind of thought. Noticing the pull to spiral down, I stopped it and entertained a much more positive thought, one of hope that it was all going to work out just fine.

As I noticed the feelings change into ones of joy and happiness, but something felt off. It was all a lie.

It was all a fabrication of the mind, neither of the feelings was real.

I contemplated my feelings once all the thoughts were removed, and there was nothing but the very familiar calm of my consciousness. But then I noticed that something else was subtly disturbing the calmness. It was some sort of pull, an urgent pull to feel at least one of the feelings. Sadness or happiness, it didn't matter which one it was, as long as there was something. Somehow the absence of emotion was not acceptable. I had to feel at least something, one way or the other, if I didn't feel anything than what was the point?

And just like that I saw the identification. The need to be something, anything would do, as long as it was something. I couldn't avoid laughing at this realization.

As the days progressed, I noticed how this activity was beyond the mere movement of thoughts, it was subtler but nevertheless very strong. I started noticing it beyond every thought, it was always there, like a curtain preventing me from fully seeing my true self.

The habit of identification runs deep and can be traced back to our young childhood, it has been with us for as long as we can remember, letting it go is not an easy task. Or is it?

The more I looked the more the mind got confused. The mind could not make sense of what I was trying to do, it could not understand the process or attempt of de-identification, so every time I went deep into my enquiry, the mind would simply shut off. I could not put two thoughts together.

With my experience I have come to understand that the mind is incapable of going to some places.

It tries very hard, but it cannot go into a realm where it does not belong. Eventually it has no other option but to rest.

My process of enquiry and investigation became more of a sense or feeling than an actual mind activity. I could sense the identification, but I was unable to analyze it or even trace it to its source, the mind just wouldn't bend that far.

What if there was no need to analyze it? What if all that was required was to sense it and drop it altogether in the now moment? No trying, no pushing, simply stopping everything.

Meaning

As the days went by, I started noticing a detachment between myself and what was happening in my life. Everything seemed devoid of meaning, pointless. I was still engaging with the world, having conversations, going places, cooking and cleaning up, but there was a feeling in me that none of it was ever going to mean anything. The more I investigated the feeling of identification, the more detached I become.

My favourite prayer, one that I had been saying quietly to myself almost every day for the past couple of months, started emerging in my mind a lot more often.

May I see the Truth beyond all illusions.

May I see only Truth.

At this point in my journey, it was the only prayer that actually made sense. So, every time I notice an illusion come up, I would repeat it to myself and be grateful for being shown what until then had been hidden.

The days coming up to my birthday filled me with opportunities to confront the illusions, but my birthday was the day where everything converged into a picture I could no longer unsee.

It was exactly 3 years since my Kundalini awakening, I woke up in a very good mood, happy with myself and the world. I had beautiful surprises, visits and presents. I had all my loved ones showing me how much they loved me and appreciated me. I launched a new book and had lots of attention and positive feedback. I had the perfect day, but still, a part of me was feeling like it wasn't enough, I had to do and achieve more. As I noticed my mind planning for the launch of my next book and sorting out plans for the new video series that were coming out, I noticed how empty I felt.

I had been appreciated, seen, valued, but still my ego was not happy.

I could see it so clearly, I could not unsee it. How ungrateful I would have sounded to anyone who could hear my thoughts in that moment. But it wasn't ungratefulness, I am more grateful for the life experiences I have then I could ever express, this was that identification I had been on the lookout for the past few days. It was strong, it was insatiable, whatever I would do with my life would never ever appease the ego's hunger for more.

I closed my eyes and went within; it was time to confront the cause of all these problems. I asked to be shown the source of these feelings and thoughts started arising. Some thoughts were just random, a pure distraction, but others were planning the next book and taking stock of what I had accomplished. I didn't fight them, instead I pushed through and went deeper. I demanded to see the source of those feelings again and the actual feeling of not enough, of emptiness, manifested in my chest. I felt it, accepted it, but it was still on the surface, I needed to go even deeper. I moved through it as if it was a cloud dissipating and went even deeper.

I noticed a heaviness in my chest, an energy that was so thick I could almost touch it. I confronted the energy, asked to be shown the source of all the commotion, and as I let my consciousness permeate it, it disappeared. There was nothing there, just calmness and quiet.

There was no source, no actual ego, no entity, just habitual thoughts and patterns that were leaving an energetic residue on their wake.

As the thoughts started slowly coming back, the mind started distracting me with the kind of thoughts that were appealing to me, it was doing everything it could not to disappear, and I seemed to be entertaining its efforts. Noticing this insane activity, I said in my own mind that I was willing to let go of everything, I was willing to die in order for my soul to live. This is when I had a very strange vision.

I saw a switch on the back of my brain. It had two different positions Ego and Soul. It was flicked to Ego, but I reached out and flicked it to Soul. As I did this, I saw a reflection of myself transform into black smoke and disappear slowly in front of my eyes. It was like the wind had come and had unexpectedly blown it all away.

After this I had an expansion of consciousness and saw how our lives don't really belong to us. We don't exist, the person never existed, only the Soul is real. I saw how quickly life passes by and how It doesn't matter what experiences we have in our lives, they are all valid, the wish of the Soul itself. I saw how we have the illusion of control and choice, but how choice isn't actually an option, the Soul has already made its choices.

This realization was really quick, lasted only a couple of seconds, but it was very intense and so clear.

As I came back to the room, I laughed. I could see beyond the illusion.

Devotion

About a week after my son and I parted ways, my internal world continued to change. I was again struggling to connect with people, I felt distant, and keeping a conversation was approaching physical pain. I had been through these same feelings before, feelings of confusion, disorientation and disconnection from people and the world, when the Kundalini first awakened in me. I was going through a new dark night of the soul.

I didn't recognize myself anymore, I no longer knew who I was, and life was becoming more and more difficult by the minute. There wasn't much left in my life giving me joy or happiness, but at least I still had David to brighten my days.

About two weeks after the fight, Kali showed herself to me again. She stared me in the eye as I was preparing to go to bed, and I knew something else was coming. No words were exchanged, just an intense stare.

As the following day unfolded, I started noticing my feelings towards David were different. I had contemplated these feelings before, but willingly ignored them. Why not? I was having fun as it was, why should I change anything? We were both enjoying our time together.

But the same way I felt compelled three years earlier to confess my love for Noah, I was now compelled to be completely honest with David. I wanted more, so much more. Unfortunately, David was unable to give me what I craved, and two days after Kali appeared, I ended our relationship.

We remained friends, our connection was very strong, and although we weren't together anymore, we still cared deeply for each other.

The confusion, the disorientation, and the feelings of being completely lost intensified after our breakup. It was a full-on identity crisis, and all I could do was trust that somehow, I would be ok, as long as I kept trusting the process, I knew I would survive.

Since the opening of the Crown chakra, the energy of Shiva was becoming very strong. He would descend every time Shakti ascended, and both energies were now very familiar to me. I became very interested in the Divine Masculine energy and extended my embodiment practices to encompass both Shakti and Shiva.

On one of my practices, as I was inviting Shiva into my energy field I felt his presence behind me, as if he was a human being. His arms were open and ready to hold me and secure me. I cannot explain in words how much love I felt in that moment, it blew me away. I felt seen, loved, held, accepted in every way. This experience lasted for about 5 minutes, and it was one of the most intense encounters I have ever had.

After this episode I started feeling like I just wanted to experience the Divine Masculine more and more, I felt like I was falling in love with that energy, a love no one in this world could possibly offer me. I actually thought that the "more" I had asked David for, just a few days earlier, was exactly what I was experiencing now. Of course, the Divine Masculine and Feminine can be experienced both within ourselves or outside with another person, we do not need to limit ourselves. But the more I dived into Shiva's energy, the more content and satisfied I felt.

I didn't seem to want a partner in my life anymore, I was feeling satisfied, seen, loved, in ways I had never experienced before. I was truly at peace with the prospect of being on my own, for the rest of my life if need be. The love I was feeling within myself was miles away from whatever a human partner could ever offer me, so I rested in that love and prospects of dating exited my mind very naturally.

In Hindu tradition, there are three paths to Liberation or Enlightenment: Jnana, Karma and Bhakti. Jnana is the path of knowledge; Karma is the path of selfless action; Bhakti is the path of Love or devotion.

In the Bhakti path of devotion, it is believed that Love is always the right answer to life's experiences and challenges. Instead of fighting them or reverting to a victim mode, whatever is being presented becomes accepted which can even lead to a feeling of gratitude for the experience itself.

Bhakti is also the desire for Divine Love, the burning love for God, which ultimately brings us to liberation. The more we practice the love and desire for the Divine in our lives, the more our system expands to be able to receive the Divine in itself.

For a bhakta, the ultimate desire is God itself, he realizes that nothing else in the world can even come close to Divine Love. And this was what I was experiencing. There wasn't a longing in me anymore, a desire for a partner seemed to be gone, I was completely in love with the Divine. Every time Shiva and Shakti manifested their union within me, I was in complete bliss, but the feeling of love and devotion accompanied me throughout the day as I surrendered to the loving energy of the Divine.

The nervous system

During one of my daily embodiment practices, I had another encounter with Kali.

As I sat in meditation, I sensed her sitting next to me. As usual, there were no words. She sat there observing me while I was in deep communion with Shiva and Shakti. After a few minutes, she stood up and with just one blow of her hand, broke my neck.

Kali is relentless, strong and beyond scary, but I learnt to trust her. I know in my heart her methods always serve my greatest good. So, I trusted her and what she was about to do. There I was completely still, feeling my head on the side of my body and incapable of moving or making a sound. I watched as she removed my bone marrow with her bright red tongue, to then replace it with golden light which appeared to be in liquid form. My neck was then restored back to its normal state and my skull returned to the top of my shoulders.

Still incapable of moving, I watched as the now golden bone marrow expanded and entered every nerve in my body. My whole body was glowing and buzzing.

Our bodies are only capable of processing certain amounts of energy, but as our consciousness expands, it becomes very difficult for the body to receive increased amounts of energy. Think of it as electric wiring. If your home has just basic appliances, the normal wires will be enough, but if you decide to install a number of new appliances and turn them all on at the same time, you may blow a fuse.

When your consciousness expands and waves of higher energy start entering the body, upgrades are necessary so that you don't blow a fuse or get seriously ill.

Kali had just upgraded my nervous system, something that Shakti had done a few times since my Kundalini awakening, although never in such an obvious or radical way.

The good news about upgrades is that when they occur, you become much more sensitive and open to receiving more of the Divine. Energy can pour in a lot quicker and in a much stronger vibration then before. I could now receive a lot more of Shiva and Shakti then previously.

My Crown was constantly tingling, energy moved constantly in different parts of my body, and I was a lot more conscious and aware of everything within and around myself. I realized that I was abiding in the realization of my true self most of the time. Every person I interacted with was shown to me as being just another version of the Universe, of me. Every situation was encountered with acceptance and seen as being absolutely perfect. The negative thoughts and feelings that came up were encountered with love and accepted for what they were, just an activity of the mind and a reaction of the body. A few times when my mind tried to bring me back to full identification with the ego, I just could not do it, I could not stop seeing me, my true self.

None of these realizations were accompanied by fireworks, every single one of them was realized in the quiet of my being, in the stillness of the mind.

The Higher Heart

Life continued moving forward without proper direction or a plan, everything seemed very up in the air. My business started failing, which brought about a sense of frustration and impotence, but that didn't pull me down for long. I quickly realized that the strong necessity to help and awaken others I once strongly felt, was now gone. Who was I to push or redirect people's lives? What entitled me to insist on people's awakening or self-development? Every person is so perfect, every single being is a perfect manifestation of the One, and I didn't want to change anyone nor anything any longer. So I closed up my business and decided to serve only those who come looking for my guidance.

At this point I met Andrew, someone very different from all other men in my past. We shared important values such as integrity and compassion, and there was something about him that I did not want to walk away from. For the first time in my life, I entered a romantic relationship without expectations, fully living the present moment and open to whatever experience would come into being. Every time we meet, he would somehow surprise me.

I worked on my fears of getting hurt and controlled, and I consciously decided to open myself up to love again. But this time was different, the neediness wasn't there, instead there was a complete acceptance and appreciation. It wasn't the conditional love I was used to, this was somehow a form of higher love. I opened myself to it, completely and with no expectations. That's when something changed, again.

One of the lessons I've learnt since my Kundakini awakening was how everything constantly changes, how attaching myself to certain outcomes, people and situations, was one of the biggest causes of my suffering. When we accept that the only constant in life is change, everything starts flowing a lot easier.

As I consciously decided to open myself to love again, lying in bed ready to fall sleep, I felt my Higher Heart Chakra open.

The Higher Heart chakra was not something I was familiar with at this point, I had heard about an extra chakra which existed between the Heart and the Throat, but never had I experienced it whatsoever. In my understanding and experience, there were the main 7 chakras, Shakti-Kundalini would travel through all of them, and once the process was complete at the Crown, Shakti would travel back to the Heart, along with Shiva, bringing the mind or ego with them. This was the end of the Kundalini journey. This was the transcendence of the ego or enlightenment.

It was a surprise for me to sense the opening of the Higher Heart. Right at the centre of the sternum bone, midway between the Heart and the Throat, also called the Thymus Chakra as it rests on top of this gland.

Again, it felt like a flower opening its petals, slowly one by one. The energy was so intense that caused a slight pain to pierce through that centre, while the whole area from my heart to my throat felt like it was immersed in warm water. I'm not sure how long this experience lasted as I ended falling asleep a while later.

After my higher heart opened up, life started moving very fast. I ran out of money and had no other choice but to go back to work in an office again. My relationship with Andrew turned out to be very short lived, collapsing quite unexpectedly.

Life was moving fast, but my spiritual practices and focus were completely still. I seemed to be too busy, distracted and exhausted to be able to sit in silence. Besides the random kundalini activity in the evening before falling asleep, it seemed like nothing was happening.

I struggled to keep my head above water and when a few weeks later I met Harry, I thought I was finally going to have a break. My relationship with Harry lasted only a few weeks, and although I wasn't in love with him, the breakup brought me to my knees. At work things weren't easy either, I seemed to have forgotten how an office environment could bring up so many insecure egos to the surface.

I had reached rock bottom several times in my life, but since my spiritual awakening, it didn't matter how horrible life may seem, I was completely convinced that nothing could ever affect me too deeply. I could always maintain that observing perspective, that sense of being a lot more than just the person. But Harry was the straw that broke the camel's back, and I dove deep into a black hole very quickly.

I tried to sit with my feelings, allow them to be safely expressed, but the mind was relentless and before I could do anything to stop it, I was beyond my breaking point. In retrospect I can see how what happen next was inevitable and even instrumental in my spiritual journey, but at the time I could not see anything, definitely not a way out.

It all started with me allowing my feelings of anger and sadness to be felt and accepted. I went through this process so many times before, sitting with my feelings was very natural to me. But on that Sunday afternoon, the process felt very unfamiliar. A despair came over me, and took control very quickly. I couldn't create any distance from the person and the suffering, I could not observe any of it. I became completely immersed in the illusion and my mind did not hesitate in taking advantage of what was happening. Very quickly the mind turned into a horrible monster, using all the realizations I had been gaining against me.

I had so many beautiful realizations over the past few years, realizations that not only brought me an immeasurable sense of peace but also liberation. All of those were now being distorted and used to destroy me. Even when I tried to cry for help all I could hear in my mind was "no one will come to help you, Maria. There is no one besides you, the whole universe is you and you are all alone" or "there is no God, there is no point" and with every thought my despair grew bigger and more out of control. I am not proud to admit that I seriously contemplated suicide. To my amazement, I did not fight the thought, I seriously welcomed it.

In desperation, I cried out but instead of asking for help, I asked God to kill me. I said I was not willing to play this game anymore, I was tired of all the suffering and all I wanted was die. I repeated over and over "I don't want this anymore, please just take me". I fell on my knees and sobbed uncontrollably for quite some time, constantly repeating "I don't want this anymore, please take me". I gave up. I simply gave up.

That's when something very surprising happened. In the midst of the despair, my mind came to a halt. In a split second I went from complete despair to total silence and peace. There were no thoughts, no feelings, absolutely nothing but nothingness. I got up from the cold floor, went to lay down and fell asleep.

I woke up the next morning still feeling nothing. There were barely any thoughts in my mind, and I remember not being sure if I had somehow died the night before or if I was still here.

This nothingness lasted for a few days, and as I came back to my normal being I noticed a few things had changed. I no longer felt the need to have a partner in my life. it had become obvious that my suffering was coming from the belief that I needed someone in my life in order to be happy, but my experience had showed me that every single romantic relationship had brought pain and suffering after just a few happy moments. My belief was so wrong, and I could not look the other way any more. The way I saw men started changing and I felt like I was becoming more self-sufficient than ever before. I felt that I was no longer reaching out, looking for solutions, I was just resting in my own centre where solutions are not needed.

I had spent several years healing my heart, it took a lot of hard work to finally open it up to the world and I was not prepared to let it close again. I had been so eager for romantic love that I forgotten that love can come in many forms. But after this episode all I seemed to want was to love.

I wanted to love life, myself, the world, everything, I wanted to love everything. So instead of reaching out trying to catch something, I seemed to be very still emanating love from every pore.

I started seeing everything and everyone as one, just part of this One consciousness, and I approached every situation and every challenge with "how can i love this situation?" or "besides the pain they caused me, how can I love them?" and I started noticing that it would take only a few seconds before I could feel love. And I don't mean just a bit or warmth towards others, I mean full on love, with my Heart and Higher Heart chakras opening and a wave of energy propagating all around me. I was now functioning from a whole different level, I started coming back to my centre, to that place of nothingness and spaciousness inside me that had no limits, I started living from that place most of the time.

There was no urgency, no worry, no suffering, just peace and love on demand. Life was happening and I was being lived without effort.

The mind would come up from time-to-time trying to bring me back to my old reality, convincing me to join a dating site or be angry with my ex-boyfriend, but I could just love all of it.

It's so incredible to see that the cause of most of my suffering my whole life became the fuel that liberated me.

This is just the beginning

As I approach the end of this book, 4 years after the Kundalini activation, I must say that the love affair between Shakti and Shiva is still active within me. I feel them almost every day, sometimes very intensely, other times just as a soft reminder that it's all still alive.

My journey has been nothing short of magic and incredibly fulfilling. I went from being completely unconscious to being aware of myself and more importantly of the Oneness that we all are. It was the most difficult time of my life, but also the most cherished and valuable.

This book was written for you. You may be just curious or have been through something similar, either way, it is specially for you. Take what resonates and let go of the rest. Remember that we are all different expressions of the Oneness and therefore we will experience things differently. This book is not intended to be a manual to follow or to leave you expecting to have the same experiences as I had, it is only a sharing of information, of experiences so you know you are not alone.

Something tells me this is only the beginning.

Printed in Great Britain
by Amazon